START YOUR OWN BUSINESS:

YOU CAN DO IT!

START YOUR OWN BUSINESS: YOU CAN DO IT!

Sue Hunter

↯

dash house
Brockenhurst
UK

First published as The Sole Trader Quick Start Handbook in 2010 by dash house.
This extensively revised and renamed edition 2014

dash house
The Croft
Woodlands Road
Brockenhurst
Hants
SO42 7SF

www.dashhousepublishing.co.uk

© Sue Hunter 2014

The moral right of Sue Hunter to be identified as the author of this work has been asserted in accordance with the Copyright, Designs and Patents Act 1988

ISBN 978 0 9567357 7 5

A catalogue record of this book is available from the British Library

Printed and bound in the UK by Lightning Source UK Ltd

Cover design by RULER

www.thisisruler.net

All rights reserved. No part of this publication may be reproduced, stored in a retrieval system, transmitted in any form or by any means, electronic, mechanical, photocopying, recording or otherwise, without the prior permission of the publishers.

This book is intended merely as a starting-point and for general guidance. It is not intended to be comprehensive, nor to provide legal advice. Whilst every effort has been made to ensure accuracy, neither the author, nor the publisher, can acccept any legal responsibility or liability for any errors or omissions that may have been made.

Contents

Introduction vii

Chapter 1
It's All About You 2

Chapter 2
Market Research 28

Chapter 3
Marketing 52

Chapter 4
Pricing, Budgeting & Cash Flow 72

Chapter 5
Keeping Records 96

Chapter 6
Your Business Plan 118

Index 137

Once again, thanks to John, David, Angela and Nick.

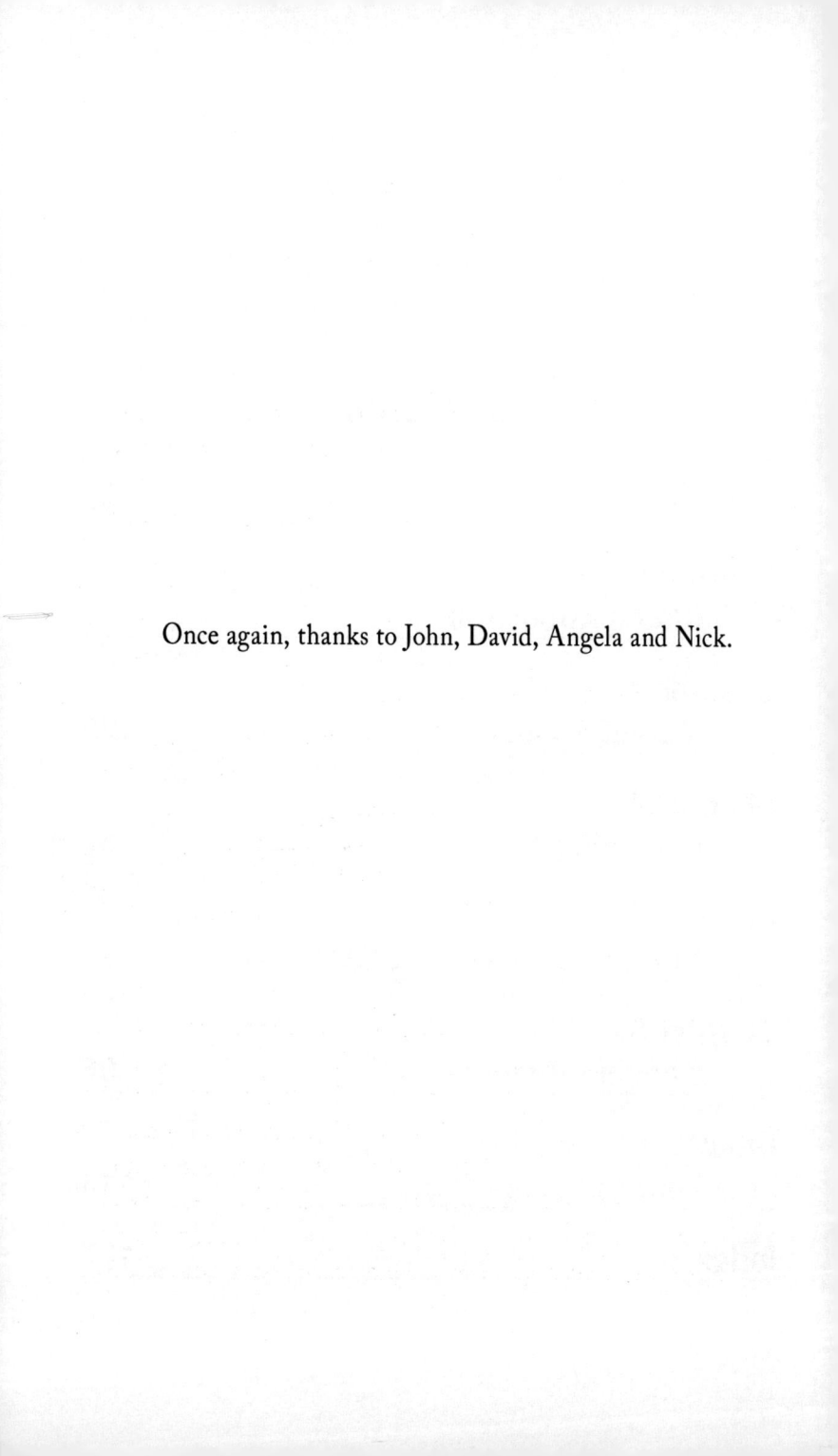

Introduction

The UK is a creative and enterprising nation, a 'Nation of Shopkeepers' according to Napoleon; an economy built on commerce and enterprise with people who were, and still are, willing to have a go at creating wealth through their own efforts and know-how. By exploring how you might start your own business you are trying to become part of this vibrant and visionary body of people who put their hearts and souls into achieving their ambition to become the owner of a successful business venture.

Not everyone is cut out for this, however, and fairly early on you should take time to examine what self employment will really mean to you and your family and whether or not you feel that you have the approach to life that will enable you to cope with the stresses and strains of business. Your ability to be resilient to small failures, yet persevere, is probably key to whether or not you will succeed.

Over half a million people start their own business each year and over half of all these will fail or cease trading within the first few months. This might be due to people realising that it is not for them, but it is also due to the difficulty of getting practical and useful advice, guidance and support. Pre-start-up agencies and Government advice sources are often not able to connect with the needs of non-business people seeking advice on how to get going. But support is vital to helping new entrepreneurs learn about how to do business, to helping you evaluate whether your business idea will work and calculating its financial viability. Too many budding entrepreneurs flounder where they could have succeeded if only someone had pointed them in the right direction.

'Start Your Own Business' is a handbook for you to learn about the basics of establishing a business and provides weblinks for you to follow-up on topics that you may wish to explore further. At this point it is important to say that if you are not computer literate and don't know how to make use of the internet to find out information then you should try to rectify this as soon as possible.

Having an understanding of how to use a computer will enable you not only to improve your knowledge about the business world, but also help you with your marketing and market research, with your accounts and with your finances. Many libraries run relevant courses for beginners, as do community-based organisations as well as colleges and 'learndirect' and you can access computers at most libraries if you don't yet have your own. If you are not convinced about this necessity now, you will be by the end of the book!

Type of business

This book is primarily aimed at people who will start their business as a sole trader because this is the legal status that is the most popular and straightforward form for start-up businesses. The legal and accounting requirements for a sole trader are relatively simple and as a sole trader you will have complete control over your business. In fact - you are the business. You will be responsible for all the debts, but also take all the profits.

Other forms of trading such as a Limited Company or Partnership are outside the scope of this book. However, much of the general content is relevant to all businesses, whatever legal framework they take.

Although, like most new businesses, you might begin as a sole trader, if your buying and selling become high in value it is worth discussing with your accountant whether or not becoming a private limited company is the right option for you.

Getting started

Often the problem with doing something new is knowing where to start. You may have an idea of where you want to go, but not how to get there. Initially with so much to sort out you may never get past the thinking stage. This book aims to help you work through the initial stages of starting your own business as a sole trader so that you give yourself a fighting chance of succeeding and growing.

What the chapters cover

As a sole trader the success or failure of your business rests with you and that is why, in **Chapter One**, you are asked to assess your own skills and abilities and start a development plan for you and your business.

Be honest concerning your motivations for wanting to be self-employed as unless you are clear about these, and satisfy yourself that they are sound, you will find it difficult to keep going when times get difficult. Will being self-employed give you the things and life you want? If so, you must motivate yourself and don't let others put you off – rather, become more determined to succeed in the face of adversity and challenges.

One of the main reasons for small businesses failing to thrive is that they simply haven't let sufficient people know that they exist and what they have to offer. **Chapter 2** and **Chapter 3** talk about how to find customers who are willing to buy your product or service and how to let them know you are 'out there'; it deals with Market Research and Marketing.

Market Research is about finding out as much as possible about your customers and competitors so that you can tailor your product and services to customers' needs and desires and win custom from competitors. It will also provide you with information about what form of advertising or promotions will attract a customer's attention and encourage them to buy from you rather that a competitor.

Marketing builds on this, as you will use the information to create an image that will attract particular customers. A marketing opportunity will be created any time a potential customer sees you, reads about you, hears about you or interacts with you. On these occasions they will either be attracted by what they experience or will be turned off. You need to make sure it's not the latter.

Chapter 4 and **Chapter 5** cover the financial aspects of running a small business and the records you should keep in order to retain control of your money, because making a profit is all about balancing your costs against your income from sales.

You need to know something about the way different costs affect your profitability in order to be able to work out when you are likely to start making some profit. Taking time to estimate when you will have to meet certain costs, and when you can expect income from sales to be received, will provide you with information you need for your Cashflow.

We work through an example of a Cashflow in chapter 4 and look at how many sales you need to make in order to start making a profit.

One bugbear of many small businesses is how to keep on top of invoices and receipts and how to account for these. Records can easily become confused, but we show you how to keep them simple and manageable. In chapter 5 we look at the records you need to keep for tax purposes and for monitoring how your business is performing against estimates. Some examples are provided. These records really don't need to be complicated, but if they start to become so then moving onto a computer based recording system will help ease the work load.

If you want to apply for a loan or other finance for your business, you will need a business plan to submit with your application to reassure the prospective funder that you have a sound business idea which will provide them with a good return on their investment in you.

Even if you do not intend to seek outside funding, you should still write a business plan as this will enable you to cement in your own mind exactly what you are trying to achieve and how you plan to do it. It will help you bring together the different activities so that they take place at the right time and so you can afford to do them when planned. If at any time your business is struggling then you can turn to your business plan and work out what's different and why you are not performing as planned. Your plan could help guide you to take the right actions to bring your business back into line.

Chapter 6 looks at the Business Plan and gives an outline of a simple example. It also covers some of the legal requirements that you need to be aware of when starting up in business.

What you probably don't realise at the outset is how exciting having your own business can be. It will give you a real sense of achievement and, if you do it right, can provide for you and your family. Remember, you don't have to know how to do everything at once; it's important to get started with doing something! Your self-esteem will grow as you tackle problems head on and learn from them. As owner and founder of your business you will be determined to do better next time. Owning your own business can help you feel in control of your life and future.

Chapter 1

It's All About You

Chapter 1
It's All About You

You may have been thinking about it for sometime but, even so, probably wouldn't make the leap into self-employment without some additional stimulus. Maybe you've been made redundant or been overlooked for promotion at work; or perhaps you now have a partner and/or family to support and want a better life for them.

If you feel 'up against it' this will help you in your determination to succeed in your own business. People who have it 'soft' generally don't make good entrepreneurs, as it's difficult for them to take the necessary risk when life is comfortable anyway. So, tune into that feeling and use it as a strength which will help ensure you keep going when others would have given up. Become an expert in your business area and you will succeed and will gain respect and self-esteem through doing so.

Look at what motivates you

Deciding to work for yourself rather than someone else could be a turning point in your life. Your reasons for this will be personal and may be a mix of:

- ❐ Believing that you can do something better than others.

- ❐ Wanting the independence to be creative in your own time and in your own way.
- ❐ Relishing the challenge of establishing a profitable business.
- ❐ Believing you can make more money working for yourself.

Try to identify what your main motivation is for going into business and challenge yourself to prove yourself right!

Over the next few months and years, once you have got started, you are probably going to make lots of mistakes and blunders and hopefully you will improve your knowledge about doing business because of these experiences. You will learn as you go and, initially, if you start with something small, within your capabilities, you will learn to do the tasks which will help you keep control of your business and you can plan to grow your business at a pace that suits you.

Facing the challenge of setting up a business is not about knowing how to do it all already, but about being keen to learn how to do business properly and being willing to put in the hours to achieve this.

All successful entrepreneurs will tell you that one of the most important lessons to understand is that you must not be afraid of making mistakes and you must learn from your mistakes. If you think that you would crumble at the first setback then self-employment may not be for you. If, however, you are willing to be realistic and honest with yourself so that you can improve your performance next time, and be determined to do so, then you have the right attitude to start with.

1.1 Business Acumen

Turning short-term opportunism into a long-term, income creating, vibrant business requires you, as the boss, to develop one very important quality — business acumen.

> **"Acumen" refers to your ability to make good judgements and decisions based on your knowledge and experience.**

To develop this you must start behaving and thinking like a business person, rather than whoever you are to family and friends. You must adopt a different persona – you're not just 'Dad' or 'Sis', 'Bro' or 'Mum' anymore; to potential customers you're the person who will offer them the service they need or the goods they want to buy.

> **'Talk the Talk and Walk the Walk' of someone who knows their business!**

Developing business acumen comes from learning and knowing about your business. If you take time to know about your customers, your competitors and the wider market place, including future opportunities, you will be able to make sound decisions that will help you develop your business. As sole proprietor you can't afford to simply 'do your thing' irrespective of the world around you. You may have a little success but it will not last and you may go out of business.

For example, you need to know about your customers' needs and preferences – think hard about what potential customers demand, do research and don't just assume knowledge;

you need to decide what price(s) to charge so that you're not underselling yourself nor pricing yourself out of the market. Competitors' prices are a good guide here, but you may choose to offer a better deal or a superior product and want to set a price to match your offer. Knowing who your main competitors are and what they are offering will help you position yourself in the marketplace and it will pay dividends to always keep an eye on what they are up to and stay one step ahead.

> **Price is important, but so also is value for money.**

Positioning yourself in the marketplace involves more than just knowing what price to charge vis-à-vis your competitors. It depends on what your particular customers regard as value for money. Commonsense will tell you that some attributes, such as good service, low prices, smart packaging or brand labels are more important to some customers than others. The trick is to know who likes what.

So, keep yourself up to date and knowledgeable about your market and know (even before they do) what your customers want and how you can beat your competitors in providing this.

> **You are the start of your business – you are the beginning of the knowledge base that will give you an edge over other businesses competing for business.**

Developing and demonstrating business acumen at first might feel a bit like developing a split personality — but gradually as you carry out your business it will become more natural. Learn about business terminology and try to understand why certain things, like business plans, keeping accurate financial records and doing market research, are important. Once you understand how these all fit into your business, your ability to make good judgements and sound business decisions will improve — and so will your chances of success.

1.2 Skills and Knowledge

As a sole trader you are your business. So, developing your business will mean developing yourself. Just think for a moment what you could offer that people will pay good money for. This could be:

- ❐ A particular skill because you are naturally talented or because you have trained or worked hard and developed a skill.
- ❐ Knowledge that you have acquired through experience or study.

I would like to be able to make this list a lot longer but when you think about it these are what it comes down to in the end — **skills or knowledge**.

These are what you must acquire in abundance if you want to be successful in business. It could be that you have a trade skill or your particular skill may be in organising other people to work as a team, or your knowledge could be about something quite limited, such as a particular piece of machinery or equipment. It doesn't matter, just so long as you recognise where and how you can use these attributes in business.

> **The more skills and knowledge you can develop and combine to make a unique offer to customers the greater your chance of success.**

You might be starting very small. Match your business with your capabilities to start with – but as you do business your personal toolkit of knowledge and skills will develop and grow. As it does, so can your business develop and grow too.

1.3 Your Personal Toolkit

Right now you might not know what you are capable of achieving, because it's not until you have some success under your belt that you will improve your self-confidence, which in turn will allow you to try new things.

> **Use what you're good at now to start your business, but be aware of what you need to develop to grow your business.**

There are some skills that will be useful to you in whatever business you start. These mainly relate to your ability to communicate with customers and potential customers; to your skills at managing the finances of your business; to your organizational abilities and to whether you are resilient to failure.

This last quality 'resilience to failure' is important because, as the biographies of many successful entrepreneurs will demonstrate, you will find that failures – either catastrophic of minor – are part and parcel of the business person's lot. You must examine your own character and decide if you will be able to bounce back from failure or whether this possibility is too much for you (and your family) to cope with.

> *How have you responded to failures and setbacks in the past? Can you face failure and come through it?*

You may also need certain qualifications, or to attend particular courses, or satisfy particular statutory requirements in order to carry out your business. For example, customers may ask whether or not you have a quality mark, such as the 'Visit England' Star Ratings for hotels and guest-houses. Customers may want to know whether you are a member of a particular trade association such as the Federation of Master Builders or be assured that you have the correct certification such as the 'Food Hygiene Certificate'. Decide if you need to achieve any of these; how important they are and when you will acquire them if you don't have them already. Can you start your business without them?

If you haven't already analysed this do a review now of your current skills, qualifications and levels of knowledge of basic business activities; think about what you are good at and what areas you might need to develop further.

It may help you to work through the 'Personal Toolkit' checklist at **Table 1 (T.1)** at the end of this chapter to start you off. Try to answer each question honestly and assess what your level is for each area. In this way you will have a starting plan to work on.

In Section 1.5 we talk about creating a Development Plan. Once you have assessed your various skills and abilities, you could transfer any actions that you think you need to take to your Development Plan.

1.4 Don't Be Afraid of Success

Even though you might be starting small this doesn't mean that you shouldn't have big ideas. Often the first step is the most difficult because it's this one that will take you out of your comfort zone. Until now you might have had a limited circle of people to associate with everyday — your family, friends and a few work colleagues. Now, you're contemplating launching your business and that will mean a whole lot more, different, people to deal with. It could be a bit daunting. If this makes you feel nervous then be reassured that most people feel this way too. Whenever we step out of our comfort zones — the ones we are familiar with — it is natural to feel nervous.

> **One of the most important qualities of successful business people is courage.**

They are not afraid to try something new and put themselves 'out there' and say 'this is me, this is what I do, judge me on my performance'. Is this you? Could it be you? Every successful business person will have had to take that 'first step' and then they will have proceeded to take another, and another, taking them out of their comfort zones and widening their horizons. This is what you must do — a step at a time. This is important, as you must be willing to put building blocks in place based on goals that you set yourself.

1.5 Your Development Plan

No one else will do it for you — it's now down to you to move yourself and your ideas forward. So, one of the first things you should do is to visualise your idea of success. What is your vision for your business and for yourself? Take a few moments to work up a vision because in the future, when times are difficult and you feel like throwing it all in, it is the desire to achieve this that will mean you persevere and not give up! Picture it in your mind:

- Why do you want to set up your own business and what is driving you to do this? Are these reasons strong enough to make you be determined to succeed?
- How will life be different when you have a successful business? What sort of person will you be?
- Where will you be working? Do you want to stay in the local area or develop a national or global business?
- Will you employ staff? When will all this happen?

Your vision for one year's time will probably be very different from that of 3 years or 5 years time. Can you imagine what the steps along the way will be? How will you have grown and developed your business?

You must be committed to your business and not just be in it for the short term; you will need to persevere, bounce back from failures and try again. Hold your vision in your head and don't look back.

> *Your vision is not a plan, it is simply a motivation; it encompasses the reasons you want to set up a business.*

In order to realize this you will need to plan your business, setting goals and deciding what needs to be done in order to attain them. Your vision – knowing where you want to go and what you want to do will help you start to form a plan.

Look at **Table 2, 'Development Plan for Sam's View Photo and Video'**, at the end of this chapter. You might draw up something similar for yourself, however rough; it's the thinking about what you want to achieve that's important. In other words — get your brain in gear! For example, at the top of the page write some aims for Year 1 and then think what you need to do in order to make sure you achieve these.

Try and write at least 3 or 4 goals and then go further and add-in what you need to do practically to achieve each goal. Write these actions into the table and decide when you will achieve them by. Be realistic as to the timescale — don't give yourself too long as it may drag on, but allow yourself sufficient time to achieve your goals.

Both goals and steps might refer to personal challenges or business targets. For example, a personal goal might be to achieve a particular qualification by the end of the year, and the steps might be to study for 15 hrs per week in preparation for this. A purely business target might be to launch your website and the steps could be finding someone to design it for you and a company to host it.

Your personal development plan will complement your business plan, which we discuss in Chapter 6. Plan your business and plan how you need to develop yourself and the actions you need to take in order to achieve your business aims.

Once you have started your plans keep them handy and return to them frequently to make sure you are on course. If you are not achieving what you planned then try to analyse the reasons for this and use this information to revise your actions in the future. It's important not to get tunnel vision, as events could be taking you in the wrong direction, so just because something has worked in the past doesn't necessarily mean that it is still effective or that it will be the best course of action for the future.

Be willing to change and don't just drift along. For this reason it is also useful to have a rough idea of where you would like your business to be in years 2, 3 and even 5 years ahead and jot down a few ideas. You can then think about the different ways of getting to your longer-term targets, changing your focus from what you are doing to where you want to be.

Finally, put a big tick in the right-hand column of your development plan when you have completed an activity. Some examples of goals and steps are given in this Table, but of course you must create your own version of this.

> *Your development plan should be your kick-start to doing business, but don't stew over it for too long and use planning as an excuse not to do anything practical!*

You need to start achieving something fairly early on otherwise you will be slow to gather confidence in your ability to do business and may never get past the planning stage. Sam, for instance, has plenty of time whilst studying to go and find himself some additional photography commissions over the summer!

1.6 Turning Skills and Knowledge into Business

Your personal readiness to become self-employed is one half of the picture; the other half is whether or not you have a good business idea; one that will make you a living and help you achieve your ambitions. This is all about finding a gap in the market.

Find the gap in the market

If you're going to offer something that other people already provide then you will need to do it 'better' than the others in order to gain customers. In the next chapter we talk about understanding what customers value and it is through understanding this that you will know how to do it better. For example, one customer, or set of customers, might demand a painstaking high quality service, but another might want a 'get it done quickly.' service.

If you can find out what customers require and can provide this, then you have the makings of a business. The gap in the market might be that you find a group of customers that want it done differently to what's already on offer. If so, do it differently and do it better.

> **A 'gap in the market' is something — a service or a product that customers need, want, or would like to have that isn't currently being provided satisfactorily.**

Here are some reasons why there might be a gap — and where there could be an opportunity for you:

- Current trends are not being met. For example, organic food becomes popular and supermarkets are slow to react.

- Current products or services are too expensive. Can you do it cheaper?

- People are bored with 'the same old thing' and want something new e.g. new styles, new activities, new food and so on. New customers might be interested. Can you make something that is currently sold to only one group of customers appealing to a new group?

- Goods or services are not being sold in the way customers want, e.g. 'I want to buy online, but can't' or 'I want this service in my home but can only get it in town'.

- Goods and services are not being delivered to the standards people want; know what these are — and deliver them.

- Something is not available in a particular location; make it available.

- You can provide something creative and different; quirky can be good — can you build a reputation for this?

Your business acumen will help you identify where the need is. Whatever you provide, however, be aware that competitors may soon catch on and want to do the same. For example, the supermarkets now sell organic fruit and vegetables at a cheaper price than perhaps you could offer. So you must always think to the future and try to estimate how long your advantage will last and what you can do to protect it. You may, for example, develop a strong brand and register a trademark, or you may quickly develop a group of loyal customers who will choose you as the preferred provider even when competitors knock at their door.

> *The secret to success here is to think about the next step before your current sales start to fall-off. Nothing stands still in business.*

So, you must keep apace with changes — in such areas as trends and tastes, in new technology and taxation as well as with other external influences, such as legislation and the threats from competition that could affect your business.

Spend a few moments to consider what the main external influences on your business might be and jot them down. Then make an effort in the future to keep an eye on what's happening in those areas and prepare to amend your business offer, or the way you do business, if necessary.

1.7 Sources of Advice and Support

You may now be at a stage where you have a good idea of what you need to do in order to get started but don't quite know how to go about achieving it. You may need to go on a course, you may need finance or just want to learn about a particular aspect of business. There are many organisations around that can help you with advice and support. Some of these are listed at the end of this chapter (**Resources**) together with website addresses for you to find out more.

Being a sole trader can be a lonely experience and it is important that you develop a network of support. To begin with you could register on the GOV.UK website https://www.gov.uk/browse/business as this will get you into the government support system for small businesses. This website includes information for businesses at all levels. One feature you might find particularly interesting, however, is the range of short videos they offer on various topics of interest to those new to self-employment.

It is important to develop a network of people around you who will support you and with whom you can discuss your business ideas. This network may include family and friends, but it is also a good idea to join a local business network where you will hear what people who are in business have to say about their experiences; you could also make useful contacts and gain knowledge and ideas.

If you do not know of any local networks try doing an Internet search for 'local business networks' in your area and see which might suit you. Some will be free but others will charge a membership fee.

1.8 Personal Debt and Attitudes to Spending

There is one more area we need to cover before moving on to the next topic, and that is personal debt. If you have high levels of debt which you are not managing to repay adequately, then, more than likely, you will have a poor personal credit rating. This in turn will mean that potential funders will be reluctant to lend you money or invest in your business because the way you manage your personal debt is a reflection of the way you will manage your business finances.

When you apply for a loan for your business, whether from a bank or other organisation, they will run a credit check on you. If your rating is poor they will not provide finance as the likelihood is you won't repay it. It is worth running your own personal credit check, whether or not you have a lot of debt, because other things can influence your rating.

For example, your rating will be adversely affected if you are not registered on the electoral roll, or if you have moved house often you can register on www.aboutmyvote.co.uk. Register all your accounts and bills to the address you give on the electoral roll and give a landline telephone number rather than just a mobile. Two credit reference agencies you could check your rating with are:

Experian

Telephone 08444 818000

www.experian.co.uk

Equifax

Telephone 03301 000180

www.equifax.co.uk

You will need to provide your address history for the past 6 years.

Having debt in itself is not a bad thing, in fact, in terms of your credit rating it is likely to be a positive if you are repaying on time, as it shows you are able to manage finances. So, deal with your debt now and negotiate to make some repayments to your creditors. For further information see: www.learnmoney.co.uk or seek advice from your local Citizens Advice Bureau or go to: www.citizensadvice.org.uk

Resources

Advertising Standards Authority (ASA)

Regulates UK advertising across all media, including TV, internet, sales promotions and direct marketing.

www.asa.org.uk

British Chambers of Commerce

Offers advice and training and run regular networking events for business owners.

www.britishchambers.org.uk/

Business Gateway Scotland

Scotland's business gateway offering practical information and help to new and growing businesses.

www.bgateway.com

Business Names Register

Check that your intended business name is available and register your name.

www.anewbusiness.co.uk

Fredericks Foundation

Provides business support and loans for start-ups to people unable to get finance through the normal channels.

www.fredericksfoundation.org/

GOV.UK

Provides information about starting-up and running a business in the UK.

www.gov.uk/browse/business

Health and Safety Executive

Offers advice and guidance on all matters to do with health and safety at work.

www.hse.gov.uk

HM Revenue and Customs

Offer tax and financial advice and guides online.

www.hmrc.gov.uk

Learndirect

Publicly funded e-learning, offering a range of qualifications but is particularly useful for English, Maths and IT learning.

www.learndirect.co.uk

Northern Ireland Business Information

Official online channel for business advice

and guidance in Northern Ireland
www.nibusinessinfo.co.uk

Prince's Trust

Enterprise training, financial support, mentoring and online guides for young people aged 18-30.
www.princes-trust.org.uk

Shell Livewire

Business advice, funding and social networking for young entrepreneurs aged 16-30.
www.shell-livewire.org

Trade Association Forum

Allows you to search for your trade association and holds discussion forums online to do with various aspects of business.
www.taforum.org.uk

UK Trade and Investment

Gives guidance to companies that intend to or are already exporting.
www.ukti.gov.uk/export

Unltd

Supports social entrepreneurs through a range of resources and information, with some funding opportunities.
www.unltd.org.uk

Young Foundation

Supports social entrepreneurs through research, discussion and investment.

www.youngfoundation.org

T.1　Personal Toolkit

All of the skills listed are useful in business. Use this table to analyse your current skills levels, your business needs and your plans to meet any shortfalls.

Starting my business — Do I have the skills I need to get started?	Weak or Strong?	Action needed?
1. Communications Skills 　a. Written (letters, advertising, forms etc) 　b. Spoken (speaking to customers, business people etc)		
2. Trade/Professional Knowledge or Qualifications		
3. Money Management (budgeting, finances etc)		
4. Self organisation (time-keeping, paperwork etc)		
5. Coping with difficult situations. (Can I handle setbacks and difficult customers?)		
6. Planning (Am I used to planning for the future?)		
7. Using IT. (email, letters, internet, databases)		
8. Willingness to try new things and experiment. (Will I be able to step outside my comfort zone?)		

T.2 Development Plan

'Sam's View' Video and Photography
31 March 2013 to 31 December 2014

Year 1 — Aims:

- ❐ To have between 8-10 regular customers in the London area
- ❐ To achieve a turnover of about £50,000
- ❐ To buy a Nikon D700 camera & AF-S 16-35mm Lens

	GOAL	Date to be achieved	Done
1	**To get x qualification**	31 Jul 2013	
1.1	Study 3 hrs per day for 5 days per week	Apr-31 Jul	
1.2	Register for exam	5 Jun deadline	
1.3	Submit portfolio	30 Jun	
2	**To develop an electronic portfolio of my work to send to customers**	1 Oct 2013	
2.1	Edit all photos	End Jul	

continued on next page

	GOAL	Date to be achieved	Done
2.2	Choose 2 videos to include	15 Aug	
2.3	Design layouts ...	Sep	
3	**Contact all theatres and Arts venues in London area**	**end Oct 2013**	
3.1	Find names and contact details for all venues	30 Sep	
3.2	Research styles and brands of each venue	1-14 Oct	
3.3	Send portfolios to each venue with customised covering note	15-30 Oct	

YOUR NOTES

Chapter 2

Market Research

Chapter 2
Market Research

What are the most important areas you should concentrate on when setting up in business? Is it the finances and the cashflow, or is it marketing and advertising, or perhaps efficient delivery and supply? These are all very relevant and during the course of this book you will find out why they are important. However, let's just think for a moment about what 'doing business' is all about.

Doing business is about:

- ❐ Being able to produce or provide something that people (your customers) need, want, or would like to have.

Fairly simple, but not the full story:

- ❐ Providing something that **customers** would like to have **and be willing to pay for.**

Getting closer:

- ❐ Providing something that **customers** would be willing to pay for and which you could provide **and make a profit**...after all, you need to make a living out of your business and hopefully a good one.

"Doing business is about providing something to customers at a profit."

2.1 Know your Customers

The most important aspect of your business — of any business — will be your customers. Don't forget this! This is where your business starts. Without customers who are willing to pay for your product or service you have no business, however good your idea. Without customers you'll not have any finances to manage; you'll have no one to deliver your goods and services to or to take an interest in your advertising.

> **Knowing about your customers, and gathering and analysing information about them, is key.**

You must work out how you can use this information to persuade them to buy from you rather than another business. The whole way you do business — the prices you charge, the promises you make, the services you provide — is your complete 'offer' to customers.

This is important because, unless you have invented something new, there will already be something 'out there' that is similar to your product or service. There may be lots of other people in the same trade or profession as you and many will be a lot more experienced and better skilled. There will probably be lots of like products on the market for people to spend their money on instead of buying yours. Many will have been around for years and will be real favourites. So why should people come to you?

2.2 Why Should People Come to You?

Customers will come to you if you can provide something that **suits them better** than what is already on the market. To know what might 'suit them better' you've got to learn about what customers value. Here are some things that might be important to different customers:

- Speedy Delivery.
- Good after-care service.
- Low price.
- Superior quality.
- Latest fashion.
- Personal attention.
- Expert knowledge.
- Efficiency.
- Quirkiness.

Often two or more of these are combined. For example:

- Young girls might want the latest fashion, but only at an affordable (low) price.
- Mature ladies might want the latest fashion **and** be willing to pay a higher price providing they get individual attention.
- Retired homeowners might value a trades person who is willing to spend time with them and understand their problems.
- Busy professionals might want someone who is quick and efficient and who doesn't talk too much.

All might be willing to pay a little more if they get the sort of tradesman, service or product they want.

> **To win customers you must understand them and their needs and meet these needs better than your competitors.**

Spend a few moments now to imagine your typical customer, or customers, and jot down your ideas of what they might require from your business. Then, when you have a moment re-examine these and think how you would satisfy customer expectations and provide reliable, excellent customer service. Imagine your customers being delighted!

2.3 Knowing is Important

So, you must find out about your customers and what they value and then decide how you can provide this. This is where you can win customers from already established businesses. If you can find out more than they know about your customers' needs and then satisfy these needs better than your competitors, then you are in business.

> **Market research will not only involve finding out about your customers, but also about what your competitors are doing.**

If there is a market for your product or service then there will be others competing for the business. If you are alone in your market then beware; do your market research and find out exactly why this is the case. It may be that there just aren't sufficient customers to enable you to turn a profit.

Gathering information and gaining knowledge may help you to recognise that you could deliver a service or product, and create your own market, in an area where customers have lost interest in the 'old' way of doing things. One example often quoted is that of Cirque du Soleil, which was founded in 1984 by a group of street performers. They recognized that the traditional circus was in long-term decline — clowns and caged animals were no longer flavour of the month and the traditional audience, children, had discovered computers!

So, the street performers did not compete for the few remaining customers but instead pulled in a whole new group — adults who were theatre goers, or who attended the ballet or opera — who were willing to pay a lot more for their 'cirque' entertainment than traditional circus customers. Cirque du Soleil creators used lots of pieces of information — to do with current customers, potential customers, costs, social trends and the competition in order to create something entirely new.

> **Your market research must not be a 'one-off' activity but is something that you should do on an ongoing basis.**

What is in fashion today might not be so tomorrow or something may happen in the wider world which will affect customer buying habits, or your competitors might do something that affects your business. You should make sure you keep up to date with these events. This 'knowing' is very important because it will help you keep one step ahead of your competitors.

Often, large companies lose sight of what exactly makes them successful. The knowledge becomes hidden within the organisation and this may prevent them from being flexible and responding to changing customers' needs. Or they may inadvertently change something within the organisation that results in losing customers because it was valued by them and no longer exists. As a small trader you have an advantage because you can stay in touch with your customers and keep an eye on the competition; you will know when opportunities arise so you can win business from those larger competitors that cease to provide what customers want.

2.4 Find your Business Model

What you will end up with, in business terms, is a business model. Using what you know about your market you will decide how best to create and deliver your product or service, what price(s) to charge, how to market your wares and your brand image. Thinking of it as a model is useful — it's the way you will do business in order to gain sales in your particular market.

What do you need to focus on to succeed?

For example, if you were promoting music gigs in a local area you might focus your business model around getting the best and most expensive DJs and latest sounds, but if this is costly and does not bring in the crowds, a reassessment might reveal that your business model should be around marketing and pricing which, if attractive to customers, will bring in the numbers which will in turn allow you to get the best DJs.

Remember 'doing business' is about providing something to customers at a profit. It is not only about finding out what customers want, but also about the most cost efficient way to get your product or service to them. If you don't think about this you could find that your costs swallow up all your profits.

Logistics

The logistics of how you do business involves deciding how and where you will get any supplies you need and how you will deliver your product(s) to customers.

Getting supplies

When choosing a supplier you will be considering such factors as price, quality and reliability. Which of these is most important for you business? Which do you want to build your reputation on? Take a few moments to think about the various materials, resources and products you will need in order to carry out your business and where you might find the best deals. Initially, price may be the overriding consideration in your decision making, but there are a few other important factors to consider:

- Do your research and try to select a few suppliers with whom you can build good relationships, especially with the key decision makers. Who within the organsation can cut you the best deal?

- Do not rely on just one supplier as they may go out of business or exert too much control over you. Have information on several so that you can keep your options open.

❐ Reliability of supply is important, as failure here may mean that you, in turn, let customers down. So, check out suppliers with others who have used them; go online and do a credit check on them to make sure they are financially sound.

❐ Don't be afraid to negotiate with suppliers, after all, you are **their** customer. Some will be more flexible than others over such things as payment, quantities and delivery options.

Getting goods to customers

At the other end of the logistics flow is how to get your product to customers, i.e. your delivery options. As with choosing a supplier, cost, speed of delivery and reliability are core factors, and again, the choices you make will depend on your business priorities and your promise to customers (e.g. "Next Day Delivery").

Your main choice will probably be between choosing either a Post Office service or a specialist courier service. The Post Office has Parcelforce or Royal Mail, both of which deliver throughout the UK and internationally. They offer a variety of different prices and delivery options depending on such things as size, weight and value of packages, speed of delivery and distances. Go to www.postoffice.co.uk for further information.

Specialist courier services present businesses with a huge variety of choices covering options for collection, delivery and tracking as well as prices for type of package. Go online and see yellow pages at www.yell.com and search for courier services. You may be able to find a local courier with whom you can discuss your particular needs and negotiate delivery prices and options. Doing this could help you keep your business overheads to a minimum.

2.5 How to do Market Research

Primary research — getting close to your customers

a) What do you know already?

If you've been working in a particular business sector or trade for a while you may already know a lot about what customers want. Just by being around them you'll have observed what they buy, what they ask for in particular, what extras they may want, what bugs them and so on. This is true whether you're a plumber or an accountant. You may not realise it but you will already have gathered useful information about customers, so take a while to analyse this and work out what it's telling you about them.

Draw up a chart and base some headings on the following:

- ❐ Customer Name and Location.
- ❐ What you know about this customer (some of their preferences e.g. very fussy about cleanliness & punctuality).
- ❐ What they bought and when.
- ❐ What kind of advertising they respond to.

- ❐ Which aspects of the service/product do they value?
- ❐ What don't they like?
- ❐ Who else do they buy my type of service/product from — and what do they think about them?

If you don't know the answers already then ask them when you next see them, or 'phone and explain that you are doing some market research and could you ask them a few questions. More likely than not, they'll be flattered to be asked. Get as much information as you can and see if you can identify any characteristics, needs or preferences common to most customers. If so, then use this information to tailor your marketing messages to them and, most importantly, to make sure you provide them with what they want.

b) Questionnaires

If you already have an idea of where to find your potential customers then it will be useful to gather some more focused information about them through compiling a questionnaire and undertaking a survey.

You might send a questionnaire to people or, even better, stand in the street or in a place where likely customers hang out and ask them the questions yourself. Yes, you have to be quite brave to do this and putting yourself and your business idea 'out there' is daunting at first, but you've got to get used to talking about your business to people, you must practise explaining what your business is all about (**See 'Making Your Pitch' in Chapter 3**) — and so doing market research in person is a good way to start.

> *Your questionnaire should be simple and only as long as necessary to allow you to gather the information you want.*

It will be easier to analyse the answers if you give people some options to choose from; however, also let them make additional comments if they would like. So use a mixture of open-ended questions (which will encourage people to explain their answers and give you information) and closed questions to which they will answer either 'Yes' or 'No'.

People will not have the time or patience to complete a long questionnaire. Give simple instructions for completing it if you are not explaining this yourself. Arrange your questions in a logical order and make the wording of questions as precise and unambiguous as possible. If you are interviewing people yourself then ask your questions in order of importance to you in case the interview is terminated prematurely. You will probably need to have a few goes at it before you have your final version, so try it out on a few friends or family, listen to their feedback and amend it.

> *When you write your questionnaire be quite clear in your own mind exactly what it is you are trying to find out and who is your target audience.*

An example of a questionnaire for someone wanting to find out if there is any market locally for gardening services is at **Table 3** at the end of this chapter. Hopefully this will give you some ideas of how to approach a simple survey. As this sole trader offers gardening services, he or she might have got permission from a garden centre to stand outside the store and carry out their survey.

Do not waste your time surveying people who have no interest whatsoever in your product or service. Go somewhere where people are likely to be interested in your offer.

c) Get a group together

Rather than interviewing people individually, you might decide to get a group of people together and either ask them questions or hand out the questionnaire and ask them to fill it in. You could specially arrange this and invite people along or, if your potential customers are likely to come from a group that you associate with regularly e.g. in the coffee bar at your local leisure centre, at a mother and toddlers group or in the pub, arrange to meet some of them and either hand out the questionnaire or ask them the questions. It might be an idea to check first with the management of the venue that they are happy for you to do this.

A group is also useful in that you can give participants the opportunity to ask questions — and these may be questions that you have not thought of. It also gives you the opportunity to turn the questions round and ask them 'Well, what would you like?' If there is some consensus around an idea then it's worth taking it seriously and investigating further.

To be meaningful you need to survey enough people to enable you to draw some conclusions from the feedback. As a sole trader try to get feedback from at least 100-150 people.

d) Wider research

Your wider market place will not just consist of customers and potential customers, but also includes those who may be your competitors, your suppliers, distributors, retailers and others, all of whom will be active buying and selling and whose activities may affect you.

Try to find out as much as you can about the market; visit trade fairs and exhibitions and talk to stall holders and customers — hand out your business cards, collect information and gather opinions; join a business network or make an appointment and go and talk to possible suppliers or outlets for your product.

Prepare a few questions or topics beforehand about which you would like to get feedback. The more you can immerse yourself in the market place, the better; this will not only improve your knowledge and help you to be innovative so that you keep one step ahead of your competitors, but enthusiasm is infectious and if you mix with others who are passionate about their business you could be inspired.

Desk research

Although questionnaires can give you high quality information about people who might buy your product or service, it will not give you much idea about your competitors or likely trends. For this you will need to do some secondary research. Begin by visiting your local library. Anyone is entitled to visit public libraries and do research.

a) Local business information

Most libraries have copies of newspapers and magazines as well as local trade and business directories. Browse these to find out about your local competition — for example who's offering what, where they are advertising, what they are saying and charging.

b) Local trade associations

Find out about your local trade association. Your library will keep a copy of the Directory of British Trade Associations. This will help you find out about what is going on in your business sector — for example if there are any local associations, newsletters, conferences, trade shows, exhibitions and so on. See also: www.cbdresearch.com/DBA.htm

c) Published market reports

You can find out about the size of your potential market, growth rates, trends and types of customers from specialist market reports. Ask you local library for any of the following:

Mintel www.mintel.co.uk for expert analysis.

Datamonitor www.datamonitor.com — covers business information across a range of industries. The service is subscription based but reports are available to buy online.

Key Note www.keynote.co.uk — gives a wide range of information about individual market sectors. Free executive summaries can be viewed online.

Information on your competition and what they are doing can be found in:

UK Kompass Register gb.kompass.com. Information includes financial data, managers and company addresses.

Kelly's Business Directory www.kellysearch.co.uk Provides a list of suppliers and their contact details.

Lexisnexis www.lexisnexis.co.uk — gives a range of articles about businesses across different sectors.

Browsing these will help you further in building up an accurate picture of what's going on in your business sector. Most libraries stock a list of these reports and may be able to provide you with summaries or extracts. Some may let you use their online service to download and print some of the pages.

d) Browse the internet

Accessing published reports will usually cost you money. However, don't forget that you can browse the internet, find out useful information by researching social networking sites. Go onto blogs and microblogs such as Twitter that are tagged with key words relevant to your business.

Join sites such as LinkedIn www.linkedin.com MySpace www.myspace.com or Facebook www.facebook.com to build up your personal profile, build up your network and connect with friends and other business people.

When using these sites transparency and honesty are very important as you can build up a long profile. Likewise, your competitors will have built their own profile and this might be very illuminating.

You can track topic trends on social networks and check for news about your sector by using Tweetdeck www.tweetdeck.com and Tweetscan www.tweetscan.com for checking what people are talking about on Twitter.

Use Technorati www.technorati.com and Google Blog Search www.google.com/blogsearch to search for key words and watch out for trends or news stories.

Try and discover what people in your target group of customers are discusing on line and what's important to them. For example, if your target market is 18-25 yr olds then follow what they are talking about, and try to understand what their concerns are. Follow bloggers that are active in your business area and have a go at writing a blog yourself for others to follow. This is a great way to get yourself known.

e) Do some 'test marketing'

If you have been speaking to people about your business idea, either through questionnaires, surveys or focus groups, then, in effect, you will have started testing out your idea and receiving feedback about it.

It would be a good idea, however, if you could also set up a limited test to sell some of your products or services before you launch wholeheartedly into your business. The results of this will help you and potential funders determine whether or not there is a market for your product or service and let you refine your offer before you invest further time and money into the business. Some examples of test marketing might include:

- Setting up a trial of one event or show, negotiate a venue, prepare an advertising campaign and run the event. This will help you find out whether you are attracting your target customers, whether it would be as popular as you thought, and enable you to discover potential problems and timings.
- Offering a limited service to a particular group of customers to determine interest, find out what they like and don't like and what other services customers may need.

❐ Selling some of your product in a defined area, for example at a music festival, fete or market stall, giving tasters and getting verbal feedback from customers.

If your test marketing is successful and indicates that there is a demand for your product or service then you should include the results in your business plan (see chapter 6) as potential funders will be interested in this; however, if you receive disappointing results use this information to think about why this was the case and to plan what you will do about it.

Choose the timing of your test marketing carefully; if your business is affected by seasonal demand, for example, avoid doing your testing out of season, however keen you are to get started!

> *Gaining knowledge isn't simply gathering information, it's using that information wisely to improve your decision-making.*

Before you launch into test marketing decide what you would call a 'success'. You need something to evaluate your results against to indicate whether or not there is a market for your business. For example, how many people would need to attend your event for it be a 'success'? How many customers would you need to promise to buy your product in the future? What value of sales would you be aiming for? Set yourself a budget for the test marketing and plan your activities so that you can gather this useful information in a cost effective way.

2.6 Don't Forget to Analyse!

There's plenty of information out there, but rather than waste effort to no purpose make sure that you use your time effectively. Otherwise you may not have any time to actually carry out your business! So, when doing market research, be sure you know:

- **What you want to find out.** Make a short list and frame your questions around each topic. Try to receive one-word answers, from a list of choices you provide, as this is easier to analyse than personal comments, but leave space for people to add their own comments as well.

- **What you have found out.** What is the information telling you? This is often the hardest part because it may not be telling you what you want to hear. For example, it may tell you that your competitors are brilliant. Don't ignore it just because you don't like it. They'd be brilliant whether you knew about it or not — but now you know you can do something about challenging them!

- **What you are going to do with the** information. The idea is to use the information to help you decide how to take your business forward. You need to decide how important each piece of information is and whether it is worth acting upon it. Do you have good evidence on which to base your decisions, or do you need more in order to be sure that it is sound? Do you need to do further research to check up on any particular aspects?

2.7 Your Market Size

Above all, your research should tell you whether there is a market for your product or service. Your potential market must be big enough for you to be able to achieve your target earnings. If there are only a few customers likely to be interested in your product or service then you probably don't have a business.

However, if your market research suggests that there are sufficient customers with **similar needs and enough spending power** for you to target, and make a profit, then you are in business.

The value of your sales, quantity multiplied by price, must be high enough in order for you to pass your break-even point (see Chapter 4).

Example market research questionnaire— Gardening Services

When you spot someone you want to interview, first catch his or her attention with an "ice-breaker", for example:

"Excuse me sir/madam, you look like a keen gardner; do you have a moment to answer a few questions to help me with my market research? I'm trying to find out what customers might like from a gardening service. It'll take no more than 5 minutes."

Whether they say "*Yes*" or "*No*", always be polite and thank them.

Q.1 Have you used a gardening service within the last year or so?

- ❒ If "*Yes*", go immediately to Q.4
- ❒ If "*No*", move on to Q.2

Q.2 Why haven't you used one?

- ❒ I do it myself.
- ❒ It's too expensive.
- ❒ I'm not interested in my garden.
- ❒ I don't know of any reputable gardeners.
- ❒ Other.

Q.3 Is there anything that might make you consider using one in the future?

If you get a negative response to Q.3, thank them for their time and finish. If they have suggested that they might use one in the future continue with Q.7.

Q.4 What did you use them for?

- ❒ Lawn mowing and or general tidying.
- ❒ Hedge trimming and or tree lopping.
- ❒ Planting and or pruning.
- ❒ Landscaping.
- ❒ Other.

Q.5 What did you like most about their service?

- ❒ They were reliable.
- ❒ Their garden knowledge and professionalism.
- ❒ They were willing to listen to what I wanted.
- ❒ They were able to do heavy work.

- ☐ They were inexpensive.
- ☐ Other.

Q.6 What did you like least about their service?

- ☐ They were unreliable.
- ☐ They didn't clear up properly.
- ☐ They didn't do what I wanted.
- ☐ They were rude/not very professional.
- ☐ They were too expensive.
- ☐ Other.

Q.7 What services are you interested in? (tick all that apply)

- ☐ Lawn mowing and care.
- ☐ Planting.
- ☐ Advice on plant selection.
- ☐ Garden design.
- ☐ Path and driveway weeding.
- ☐ Water features.
- ☐ Border development.
- ☐ Garden tool sharpening service.
- ☐ Any other?

Q.8 How often would you use this service?

- ☐ At least once per week/weekly.
- ☐ At least once per month/monthly.
- ☐ Every few months.
- ☐ Once per year.
- ☐ Other comments.

Q.9 How much would you be willing to pay for a professional gardening service?

- ❐ Under £75 per day.
- ❐ £75 to £100 per day.
- ❐ £100 to £150 per day.
- ❐ £150 to £200 per day.
- ❐ More than £200 per day!

Q.10 Where would you normally look to find out about a gardening service?

- ❐ Local newspaper.
- ❐ Internet.
- ❐ Local shop card displays.
- ❐ Leaflet through door.
- ❐ Word of mouth.
- ❐ Other.

"Thank you very much for your time. Here is my business card. May I have your contact details?" (Note them down!)

YOUR NOTES

Chapter 3

Marketing

Chapter 3
Marketing

Marketing is an investment in your business that will reap rewards over time. It is the whole process of how you persuade people to buy from you rather than from your competitors. It involves informing, enticing, persuading, reassuring, engaging and retaining customers. Unfortunately it is something that many small businesses do not do well.

> **Poor marketing is one of the main reasons why start-up businesses fail.**

Marketing is all about how you will 'sell' your business to customers. Although marketing covers the whole range of devices used in order to persuade customers to buy a product or service, the 'selling' part is often thought of as that face-to-face or 'over-the-phone' activity that lots of people dislike. Sole traders find it difficult to do and customers shy away from persistent and pushy sales-people.

However, 'selling' need not be a problem either for you as a sole trader or your customers if you understand your business, and can talk about it enthusiastically, and know enough about your customers and potential customers to be able to explain to them how they will benefit from buying from you. Let's look at this first.

3.1 It's All About Customer Focus

As a small business you will find it very difficult to compete with larger, well-resourced organisations unless you use your knowledge wisely. But you do have an advantage because you can get close to your customers and you should aim to use your particular strengths to provide what you know your customers value. You must focus on a particular market and get to know it well.

Once you have found out as much as you can about your target customers you can decide how best to promote your business to them. Try to create a picture in your mind of your typical customer and what matters to them. If you are unable to do this then you need to do further research. Analyse this information so that you can create a business offer that is uniquely relevant to them. You must try to look at things from their point of view and not from yours!

> *Your Unique Selling Point, or USP, will set you apart from your rivals, but it will only attract customers if the USP is valued by them.*

Take a few moments to write down everything that you think is important to your customers. Next work out how you can promote your business so that your marketing materials show that you know what is important to them **and** why they should buy from you. This is often referred to as 'selling the benefits' rather than just the features of a product. But what does this mean?

3.2 Selling the Benefits

The features of a product or service are to do with the facts about it, e.g. quality, size, ingredients, colour, method of delivery, reliability of service and so on. And once you know which of these are important to your customers, in your marketing, you must turn it round and sell the benefits i.e. how will these features benefit your particular customers? It may be interesting to customers that you say for example 'we are proud of our reputation for high quality craftsmanship' but so what? What will be the benefit of this to the customer? After describing a feature you must follow with 'which means...' and then say what it can do for your potential customer.

If you are setting up a tanning salon, the features of your offer are that customers will get an all-over tan without any sunbathing. But what will this mean to your typical customers who might be young females or males? It might mean that they will look good on holiday, which might mean they will have a holiday romance, which might mean they will find a lifelong partner — or just have a great time and get lots of photos on Facebook for their friends to see. A good tan could boost their self-esteem. Imagine the kind of advertising you would use to promote this aspect of the benefits.

> *How could you use the knowledge about your customers to make your 'offer' stand apart from your competitors'?*

If you were selling electric drills your market research might have told you that your main customers were family men. A drill will not only make a neat hole in the wall but also will bring the customer satisfaction because it will mean he can build those long awaited bookshelves and sit in his favourite chair to admire his collection.

> **Always think 'what does this mean for my customers?' ... and then tell them!**

Before you start marketing, therefore, you must know what benefits will be important to your customers and then ensure that everything your business does shows that you understand your customers better than your competitors do and you can provide all the little extras that you know will mean a lot to your customers.

3.3 Your '30-second Pitch'

If you are talking to people directly you will need to be able to explain in very few words exactly what your business is all about. You have to engage their interest in the first few seconds, enough to make them want to hear more. There will probably be lots of opportunities for you to sell your business using only a few moments of someone's time. You need to think about those important aspects of your business that will grab the attention of others and make them sufficiently interested to follow-up.

Try and write something now and refine it as you learn more about what is important to your customers and what makes you different from your competition. In three sentences you could say:

- ❐ Your name and the name of your business and what you do.
- ❐ What makes you special and different to your competitors; this might be a special service you offer, the materials or processes you use or the added extras you provide, and so on. Remember — whatever it is, it will only make you special if it is valued by your customers.
- ❐ How this benefits your customers. "This means that ..."

Try to make your pitch meaningful, that is, don't use clichés such as 'excellent customer service' or 'quality product'. Finally, keep your pitch simple. If the listener is interested they will ask for facts and figures and you can continue the conversation — but first you must get them interested!

> **Remember, you are trying to make yourself stand out from the competition and demonstrate that you have something special to offer.**

You must be able to explain your business offer to people and so you should practise your sales pitch — in front of a mirror or to family and friends — until you are confident. Use what you know about your customers to show them how buying from you will be a benefit to them. Have your information to hand:

- ❐ Know all the features of your product or service.

- ❏ Be able to explain simply the main benefits.
- ❏ Answer any likely objections.
- ❏ Say why you are better than competitors.

Have all this information ready so you can give your sales pitch at an appropriate time and feel comfortable doing this. Do not use jargon unless you are sure the listener will understand this; rather, explain your business using language to suit your customers. It is important that you show that you believe in your product and demonstrate your enthusiasm. If you don't believe in it then no one else will either. So, give it your best shot but if the customer is still not convinced then don't be too pushy. Remember, listening to what the customer is telling you is more important than bombarding them with information.

3.4 Sales Checklist

Here are some tips to help you with the sales process:

First Impressions

Be on time, dress for the occasion, smile, greet and make eye contact.

Build Rapport

Everyone likes to talk about the weather — mention it! Compliment customers; say, for example, "You have a lovely home!" People will then think you are similar to them and have the same tastes or style.

Questioning

Ask open questions, ones which will require them to say more than a 'Yes' or 'No'. Rather than asking 'Do you like this kind of music?' you could ask 'What music do you listen to?' Open questions start with 'What', 'Which', When', 'Where' etc.

> *Part of 'selling' is listening to what people are telling you. Listen more than you talk!*

Presentation

Listening will help you get a feel for what is particularly important to your customer then you can say what your product or service will do for them, e.g. save them time, make them look good.

Listen for buying signals

A customer may make up their mind to buy before you've finished your pitch. Listen for these 'buying signals', e.g. they may say 'When can you deliver by?' or 'I like the blue one'. If they do then stop 'selling' and close the deal.

Closing

Once you've been chatting for a while you should test whether you have made the sale by attempting a trial close. Close the deal by asking for the business, for example by saying 'how many would you like?' or 'shall I wrap that one for you?'

Thanks and Follow-up

Thank them for the business. Ask for a referral or think of another way to achieve follow-on business from your current customer.

3.5 Your Marketing Plan

The best way to win and keep customers is to set out a simple Marketing Plan. This should cover:

- ❐ **How you will attract new customers** — this may include doing some advertising in your local newspaper, leaflet drops, giving presentations or setting up a website. Which method(s) do you think would bring in the most customers?

- ❐ **How you will sell more to current customers** — you need to let your current customers know what else you could do for them; perhaps include the information with the next invoice. Do you know what else might interest them?

- ❐ **How you will retain loyal customers** — show you value their custom by offering them discounts or sending them a newsletter? What other incentives could you offer them so that they keep coming back to you rather than go elsewhere?

- ❐ **When you will do each activity** — When can you afford the money to pay for them? When would be the best time to do your marketing? You not only need to decide when your customers will be most responsive, but make sure you have the ability to respond to customer enquiries should they come flooding in. It would be poor business to generate enquiries and then not get back to people promptly.

> **Your marketing plan does NOT need to be complicated – it's simply a guide to help you decide what methods to use and when to use them, and to find out exactly what each will cost so you can budget for them.**

So that you don't waste money keep a record of the response you get from each activity and how many customers it brings to your business and adjust your plan accordingly. This will help you avoid the pitfall of spending a lot of money on badly targeted marketing; instead you can spend on what works.

3.6 How to Reach Your Customers

Advertising is one form of marketing your business. It's the bit that usually costs you money. However, every time you interact with a customer or every time they hear about you or see you, there will be a marketing opportunity. This hopefully will be a positive experience for both you and your customer, but if you do not pay attention to your image at all times, then it may be negative marketing experience and harm your business rather than benefit it.

So, marketing starts with deciding what image you wish to present to customers and then ensuring that this is carried through to every aspect of your business — to your dress style or uniform, to your manner of dealing with customers, to your literature and marketing message, to the car you drive and the promises you make to customers. The total is known as your 'brand'.

> **Your brand is your promise to your customers and it is a promise that you must live up to.**

Never over-promise and under-deliver, rather, promise what you know your customers want and then delight them by delivering an even better service or product. This is how you will be remembered and how you can gain competitive advantage over your competitors.

Once you are satisfied that you have got your image right you may want to design and register a trademark in order to distinguish yourself from your competitors. Your trademark should be distinctive and provide a graphic image which customers and potential customers will recognize immediately as your business.

> **Marketing yourself and your business is an ongoing, ever present activity.**

Your trademark can be comprised of words, numbers, designs or a combination of these. The way to register your trademark is to apply to the Intellectual Property Office online at ipo.gov.uk. Before choosing a trademark for your business it is wise to undertake a search online to determine whether or not it is acceptable as certain rules and regulations apply as to what you may and may not use or say. Use the website to carry out your investigations as well as to register.

3.7 Building Customer Loyalty

Once you have customers you don't want to lose them. It is important to keep reminding them that you understand their needs and can offer them solutions to their problems. Your competitors will always be 'knocking at the door' so you must give your customers reasons why they should stay loyal to you. Don't let them forget why they bought from you in the first place and educate them about the benefits of buying from you through such things as newsletters, special offers, open days or competitions. These are all tricks of the trade used by successful businesses to maintain customer loyalty.

> **Make your customers feel appreciated and important.**

Thank them for their custom after each purchase, and you could ask them if they would like advance information of special offers or new products or reward their loyalty through discounts and special deals. Ask for their feedback and let them know that their opinions count. Remember a satisfied current customer is more likely to buy from you than someone who has not bought before.

Loyal customers are often the source of new business so consider including a request on every invoice to the effect: 'If you like what we've provided please tell your friends about us. Thank you', or think about some other novel way to encourage them to let others know about you. Look after your good, loyal customers and politely distance yourself from your troublesome ones. This could save you a lot of grief!

> **Experience shows that 80% of your problems in business will be caused by 20% of your customers.**

As the boss of the business you can choose with whom you do business and, quite simply, if you do not like a customer you do not have to deal with them.

3.8 Advertising

From time to time you may need to pay for advertising, but, before you do, decide exactly what you hope to achieve from this in order to get best value for your money. So, before choosing the advertising media, think about which group of people you want to reach and what you want them to do as a result of the advert; then decide which will help you best achieve your objectives.

Your market research should have given you a good idea of what specific media your target customers pay attention to — which papers and magazines they read, whether they read professional newsletters, how often they use the internet, what radio stations they listen to, what TV they watch, the type of mail they open and read, whether they look at notices in local shops etc. Lots of homes also receive local parish or community magazines which carry advertising for local businesses at very reasonable rates. Decide which media to use and when to do your marketing in order to reach the right people at the right time.

Your advert may be the first thing a potential customer learns about you. If you are not confident at putting together a catchy, well laid out and correctly spelt advertisement, then do make sure you get someone, whose advice you trust, to check it over for you before you blunder or just waste your money. Here are a few tips for writing your adverts:

Keep it simple

You may decide that a simple one-page flyer is the best way to get your message to customers. A useful rule to follow when designing and writing this, as with most adverts, is know as **AIDA**:

- **A**ttention. What will grab the attention of your prospective customers? Make this stand out clearly and simply.

- **I**nterest. You've done your market research so you know what elements of your offer will be important to your customers. Stimulate their interest by mentioning a couple of them.

- **D**esire. Remember, it's not really the features that you're selling, but the benefits "which mean …" that if they buy from you they will satisfy some desire. Show this desire being satisfied.

- **A**ction. What do you want to achieve as a result of the leaflet or advert? Do you want customers to phone, to look at your website, visit your shop? Is there a coupon they should cut out and return for a special offer? Be clear about this.

Above all, don't forget that advertising is part of your overall brand. What general impression do you want to convey? Will it be classy? Will it be cheap and cheerful? Will it be knowledge based or perhaps reassure customers as to your technical competence? Think how you can carry this branding through to everything you do, say or write and use appropriate language and images to convey this.

Advertising Online

Every businessman or woman should consider using the power of the Internet to promote his or her business as this can be very cost effective. However, as with all marketing you must have a clear idea of what you hope to achieve. Some methods include:

Online directories — even if your business only serves a local community at the very least you should consider having your business details included in online directories, such as Thomson or Yell. (See www.thomsonlocal.com and www.yell.com)

Develop a website — a website will give you the opportunity to promote your brand and show in words and pictures why customers should buy from you. It is your shop front and should communicate everything about your business concisely and attractively. Make it easy to find and, unless you are already adept, you should employ a professional to design and structure your website and make sure it appeals to your target market. They could also help you with search engine optimisation and keywords to ensure that you will be high up on the search engine pages like Google and Yahoo.

Social Media Marketing — social networking sites are a great way to get your name out there on the internet. You have unlimited opportunities to post links to your website, blogs, articles and so on. Use them carefully to drive traffic. Social media marketing is much more personality based and personal than printed marketing material. You can give your followers interesting, useful and well-timed material.

Pay-per-click — allows you to place an advertisement on a search engine results page and only pay for the advert when someone clicks on it. You do have to pay up front for the keywords, however, and this can be expensive. There are a number of PPC service providers that you can choose to host your advertising, including Yell Direct, Google Adwords, Yahoo! and Facebook. There are also tools that you can use to generate keywords. One example is free from SEOBook http://tools.seobook.com/keyword-list.

eNewsletters - if you are able to produce good standard written material then try creating a regular eNewsletter for your existing customers and to attract new ones. Your newsletter must not be waffle; it must contain material that is of interest and value to your customers such as advice and information, special offers, competitions, news of events and new products or services. Look at it from the point of view of your target audience and imagine what would interest them.

Email newsletters could offer you the ability to track who opens your enewsletters, what links they click on and what content they read. They will allow you to measure how readers respond to your content. Make sure you give visitors to your website the opportunity to enter their email address to receive a free newsletter and advice and include this in all your publicity material.

Conversion rates

Whichever advertising method you choose you should always measure the success and track what works and what doesn't work, otherwise you might be spending money uselessly. You could:

- Add a code into the advertisement that you ask customers to quote.
- Ask customers about how they heard about you or where they saw your advert.
- Provide a hook that customers have to act on such as cutting out a voucher from an advertisement to receive a discount or free item.

For further information, help and advice about marketing for small businesses, including internet marketing, see the Marketing Donut website at www.marketingdonut.co.uk

3.9 Customer Care

It is often said that there are two rules to good customer service:

- Rule 1. The customer is always right.
- Rule 2. If ever you believe the customer is wrong refer to Rule 1!

Studies show that while a customer who has had a good experience will tell one person about it, a customer who has had a bad experience will tell nine or ten people — or if it gets discussed online — many, many more.

If a customer complains about your product or service make every effort to deal with their complaint quickly and politely. Complaints can help you pinpoint problems with your business, and so it is important to take notice of them and act upon them. Your policy should be to:

- ❐ Take careful note of the complaint.
- ❐ Apologise sincerely for the problem.
- ❐ Investigate the complaint fully.
- ❐ Offer a replacement product, a refund or credit note.
- ❐ Make a follow-up call or letter to ensure that the customer is now satisfied.

Your customers have a number of legal rights that you should be aware of. These rights apply whether they bought something in a shop, by mail order or online:

- ❐ If you sell a product that is faulty the customer is entitled to a full refund.
- ❐ If a service is not provided with reasonable care and skill, within an agreed timescale and for an agreed price, customers can ask for a full or part refund.
- ❐ If you sell goods by phone, mail order or over the internet, customers have the right to a 'cooling-off period' during which they are entitled to change their minds and cancel the order.

The Office of Fair Trading provides guidance on customers' legal rights — see www.oft.gov.uk. Businesses that hold information on individuals must also comply with Data

Protection Act 1998. For further information see the Information Commissioner's Office website at www.ico.org.uk.

All businesses have a duty to ensure their advertising is legal, decent, honest and truthful. You can get further details from the Committees of Advertising Practice see www.cap.org.uk.

3.10 You Lead Your Brand

Marketing is all about getting your message out to your current customers and prospective customers. Advertising is one form of marketing but everything you do, say or write is part of your marketing and some of it will be planned and some unplanned. So, you need to be aware that as a business you are in the public eye and try to make sure that your brand image is consistent.

> *If you have a good product or service to offer there will be people out there who would welcome the opportunity to buy from you.*

Don't be afraid to talk about your business and don't be afraid to sell your business to customers. Show them you know what they want and how you can provide it; in that way you'll be doing them and yourself a favour.

YOUR NOTES

Chapter 4

Pricing, Budgeting & Cash Flow

Chapter 4
Pricing, Budgeting & Cash Flow

In Chapter 2 we learnt that "Doing business is about providing something to customers at a profit". Vital to this, of course, is having customers who are willing to pay for your goods or services, but another critical aspect is to control the costs so that you do actually make a profit.

Your sales will bring in income at certain points throughout the year but you must ensure that you have sufficient money coming into the business **at the right time** in order to pay your bills. Calculating when, and from where, money will come into your business and when it will go out is what budgeting and cashflows are all about.

> *Money flows are not something that just happen — you control them.*

4.1 Costs

Unless you control your spending right from the start there is every liklihood that your business will not survive more than a few months. So, pay attention to your costs from the outset; your survival will probably depend on it.

Go online and find the best bargains and free stuff — the high street banks are a good starting point for this, and many offer free advice and software. Keep your office set-up costs low by looking at web sites such as www.gumtree.com or www.emmaus.org.uk for furniture and fittings. If family and friends will help you out for free — then use them, or barter with other small businesses and swap goods or services rather than paying for them.

> **The bottom line here is — do not incur a cost unless you absolutely have to!**

Rather than paying for advertising explore how you can get some for free; for example, are you up to doing a radio interview, writing an article for the local paper or writing a blog? Could you offer some of your product as a raffle prize and gain interest that way? Use word of mouth by talking about your business whenever you get the opportunity. Think creatively, and, before you pay for anything, always consider whether it's the most cost effective way to do business.

All your costs relate to things that are going on in your business. These costs fall into three categories:

- Start-up costs
- Variable costs
- Fixed costs.

a) Start-up costs

At the outset, work out what you think your start up costs will be. So, for example, these may include the purchase of equipment or some form of transport, or an initial supply of raw materials or purchase or lease of premises. Make a list of these costs and be as accurate as possible; do your research to make sure you know what you will have to pay and whether this will be 'up-front' or whether you can negotiate spreading the cost throughout the year. Make a note of when you will have to make the payments. This will help you determine whether you need additional finance to get you going.

b) Fixed Costs

Once you have done most of your research for your business you will need to decide on your business model, essentially:

- How you are going to make your product or deliver your service.
- Where you are going to operate from.
- How you will get your product or service to market.

Setting up your business, even without any sales, will mean that you will incur some ongoing costs such as:

- Advertising and Promotion.
- Vehicle Maintenance.
- Printing, Postage, Stationery.
- Phones, including mobile.
- Equipment costs.
- Utilities e.g. heating, lighting.
- Rent and rates.
- IT costs.
- Interest on loans and overdraft.

❐ Professional fees.

Note that none of these costs are 'money earners', that is they are not directly related to your making or selling the product or service and will not necessarily result in sales. For this reason they are known as 'overheads' (or fixed costs). It is important that you keep a tight control of these and make sure that expenditure is necessary before committing yourself.

> *Your cashflow forecast is simply an estimate of when you expect money to come into the business (income) and go out (expenditure).*

From the outset you should estimate how much you plan to spend in each area and when you plan to spend it. Decide on a budget for each and then try to stick to it. Group your main area of expenditure under budget headings. These amounts will also be included in your cash flow.

What you take out of the business as your pay (personal drawings) will be part of your fixed expenses and you should work out how much you will need each month to live on. This is called your Personal Survival Income (PSI) and you should include everything you need for yourself and your dependants including such things as all household bills, entertainment, clothing, food etc. Once you have estimated your total monthly financial needs you should then deduct from this total any income you receive from other sources. The result will be what you need to make from your business in order to meet your personal living requirements. These monthly amounts will be included in your cash flow as 'drawings'. An example for Sam is included at the end of this chapter in **Table 4**. Have a look at it and try to do your own calculations.

c) Variable costs

If you have to buy goods, materials and/or services in order to make sales, these purchases, or costs, will vary according to the volume of business you do. For example, if you make and sell an evening dress for £100 but the cost of the material, thread and other decoration was £50 then the variable cost of your sales will be £50 per £100 of sales. Put another way, the variable cost of your sales will be 50% of your sales value.

Variable costs might also include contract labour or casual labour needed either to produce the goods or fulfil services or delivery costs.

It is important that you set the right price for your goods or service. If you pitch your price too low you may not be covering all your costs and if you pitch it too high you may not get anyone to buy at the price.

4.2 Setting a Price

There is no precise science involved when deciding the optimum price for your product or service. As with most aspects of business it is your business knowledge, about such things as competitors' prices, customer preferences and the wider state of the market, that will help you achieve the right outcome. You will probably have to experiment a little with different prices before you feel that you're charging the right price for your goods or services. There are, however, certain guidlelines to bear in mind when determining price.

a) "Cost Plus" method

This is where you work out all your costs and then add a percentage mark-up to allow for unforeseen expenses and to provide a profit. You must know your costs in order to make sure your price is high enough to make a profit but your price should also reflect the value your customer places on your goods or service. If this value is less than what it costs you to provide the product or service, you don't have a business; if it is higher you could be underselling your product if you base your price solely on cost plus a percentage profit. So to do this in isolation, ignoring your competitors' prices or how much your customers might pay, is not a good idea. Pricing your product or service too low is best avoided because raising prices later is difficult and may lose customers without good justification for this.

b) Perceived value

Your market research will have given you a good idea of what prices your competitors are charging and this is the starting point for setting your own prices. Could you charge more by providing something that your customers value which is not offered by your competitors and does not cost you a lot to provide?

Understanding perceived customer value will help you recognise those aspects of your business which are important for you to excel at. For example, one group of customers, perhaps those that live in rural areas, may think that it is important to have good after sales service, but others, maybe town dwellers, are not so bothered about this because they can access repair and DIY shops easily; to this group, perhaps speedy delivery is more important. If different customers value different things you will need to assess whether it is worthwhile trying to provide what each group would like, or if this is not practical, then concentrate on providing an excellent service to the group that will bring you the greatest profit.

> **Perceived value refers to those product features valued by a group of customers.**

You can find out through social media and the press what your competitors are doing well and what they don't do so well — you could copy the better features and use what they don't do well to steal an advantage over them. For example, if they appear unreliable make sure that you are reliable and promote that aspect in your advertising literature. What you are really setting a price to is your total 'offer' to customers — this is the sum of everything you are offering. This will include not only the basic product or service but all the additional benefits that you might include such as speedy delivery, excellent warranties, technical support, wide choice, personal service and so on. But these will only attract a higher selling price if they are important to your customers.

c) Undercutting

Alternatively, you may decide to undercut your competitors and try to gain business that way. You might focus on keeping costs to the very minimum; your additional benefits to customers might be almost nil — and if your market research has shown that this is what your customers want, i.e. low price with few frills, then it could be the right option for you. However, be aware that it might trigger price-cutting by your competitors and:

- a downward spiralling of prices in which no one wins.
- no profits are made.
- you must cover your costs and make a little extra to put back into the business.
- low price might be associated with low quality in the mind of the customer and make it difficult for you to improve your image and increase prices later.

d) Discounting against a high price

If you want to maintain your brand image as high quality/high price you could choose to compete by offering special price discounts or special promotions, whilst keeping the 'normal' price high. You could use this option to offset seasonal variations in the demand for your product or service or use it to win customers who normally use a cheaper competitor.

You might need to experiment with prices and see what effect lowering or raising the price has on your sales. Raising your price could lead to a fall in sales volume and lowering them could increase sales — but by how much? Again, the answer is in knowing your customers and how they will respond to price changes.

Once you begin trading you will have to meet your costs. Calculating them, therefore, means firstly estimating your sales.

4.3 Estimating Sales

Once again, your market research should provide the information you require here. From your research you should have a good idea of the potential for sales and be able to make an estimate of how long it will take you to grow these sales. Do not make the mistake of just assuming that sales will be there, that people will automatically buy from you rather than someone else.

To start with make sure you have a good idea of where your customers will come from and how you will deliver your product or service to them. Then, in order to get a realistic estimate of how many sales you might achieve, answer these questions:

- Are any of these likely to be 'big', high value, customers and how often will they buy from you?
- How many smaller customers do you think you will achieve?
- How many of these are definite customers?
- How many have expressed an interest in your product or service but will need additional input from you in order to ensure a sale?
- How many 'others' do you think are out there who, with a bit of persuading from you, might buy your product or service?

These are the kinds of questions you need to answer when trying to estimate your sales. Answering them will also help you determine how much work and expenditure you will need to commit to in order to bring the sales home.

Try to set yourself some sales targets for a particular period and plan your advertising and other marketing activities to direct your efforts and help you achieve your targets. You must think where your sales will come from and be confident that you will be able to manage the sales, i.e. deliver on time and deliver the service you promised. It is best to grow your business slowly, and learn about the problems and realities of producing and delivering a product or service before going after new business which you may not be able to find.

When estimating sales, work out how much business you think you can achieve in a typical week and estimate the value of this. As most businesses have good times and low, often due to seasonal fluctuations, also estimate what you think a good week would look like as well as a bad week. Take these amounts and multiply up to show estimated sales for a typical (average) month, a good month and a bad month.

Your fixed costs plus your variable costs give you a figure for your total costs. This information, together with your estimates for the value of your sales, gives you the figures to plan your cash flow for the forthcoming year.

What are the particular costs associated with delivering this volume of sales? Of course, your variable costs figure will be an estimation, it won't be precise, but that doesn't matter, just have a go at trying to work out all the costs involved.

4.4 Cash Flow Forecasts

Cash flow forecast is an estimate of when you think you will receive cash into your business and when you will have to pay it out. It is important because it is the measure of your ability to pay your bills as they become due for payment. It depends on the timing of the amounts of money flowing into and out of your business each week and month. The aim is to keep the money flowing in and out of your business, and build a reservoir to retain some as it flows through your business.

At the end of the chapter is an example of a completed cash flow which is explained below. You can copy this example and insert headings for your main areas of expenditure in the left hand column instead of using Sam's. To start with use a spreadsheet for your cash flow, but later you might consider using a simple accounting package such as **Money Manager** from **Moneysoft**.

Cash Flow for 'Sam's View' (See Table 5)

Sam is setting up as a freelance Video Photographer. He is going to focus on producing videos for Corporate Clients and Performing Artists. These are his two main income streams.

The cash flow has 12 columns, one for each month covering the first year of business. It also has a column labelled **'Pre Start'** where Sam has worked out how much he will need in order to get started and to cover him until he is established. He is going to borrow £1500 from his mother and repay her over the year at £130/month which will give her some interest on the loan. He is also going to put £1500 of his own money into the business. **CASH IN** is shown at the top of the page and **CASH OUT** is shown underneath this. The calculations showing whether Sam has more coming in than he has going out (Net Cash Flow) is shown in the third line from the bottom and opening and closing balances for each month are shown below these.

Let's look at cash sales into the business. Under 'Quantity of Sales' Sam has estimated likely income from his work with corporate clients and with performers for the year and entered figures for each month. The income is included in the cashflow in the month he expects to receive it whether or not this is when he carries out the work. He reckons that income from corporate clients will fall significantly in January because of reduced business in December but income from performers will increase in January as a result of more business activity in December.

> **Note that he estimates a month's lag between doing the work and getting paid.**

Cash out of the business includes figures for all the costs that we have talked about in Section 4.2. You will see that Sam has calculated his monthly outgoings under his main expenditure headings shown in the left hand column.

The first costs to enter are the 'start-up' costs and Sam has calculated that these will be about £2,045. The next costs to enter are the 'fixed' costs or overheads; i.e. estimates of costs that are incurred whether or not you do any business. Sam has included in his cashflow fixed costs for business rent and rates, advertising and promotion, phones, stationery, vehicle costs, insurance and loan repayment.

The other costs to include in the cashflow are 'variable' costs; i.e. costs that vary according to the volume of business. Sam plans occasionally to use the services of a contract photographer and these costs are shown under 'Sub-Contractor/photographer'.

His own drawings will vary according to profit made and his personal needs. Sam reckons he needs to draw a minimum of £800 per month to live on. But as soon as he thinks the business will stand it he aims to increase this to £1500 per month and then £2,000 per month. He has also estimated the amount he will have to spend on supplies each month in order to fulfil the orders for the following month. He estimates that supplies will cost about 1/10th of the value of his sales.

The bottom line shows Sam that he is likely to be in deficit in the first few months of business and so he will arrange with his bank manager for an overdraft facility sufficient to see him through this period. By the end of the year, however, he estimates that business should have made a profit of £14,491 to carry forward to the next year.

4.5 Managing Your Cash Flow

The secret to ensuring that you 'stay liquid', i.e. that you have sufficient cash to pay your debts when they are due, is to keep control of your flows of cash into and out of the business. Some ways to manage these are:

Set up your systems at the outset

Prepare your budgets and cash flow forecast in advance of each year's trading and then during the year review your progress against your estimates on a regular basis — at least once per month. In your cash flow add another column to the right of each month where you can add in the actual figures for that month as and when you have them. Once you have this information you must use it to plan for the future and take any actions you need.

> *Your cashflow is a forecast of what you expect to happen. You also need to track month by month what is actually happening.*

Control your income

Be careful how much credit time you give to customers — allowing customers to pay sometime after they have received the goods or service will cost you money. Define your payment terms before they buy. These could be Cash with Order (CWO); Cash on Delivery (COD); payment after a certain period e.g. 7 days or 30 days. You could offer a discount for early payments or other incentives to encourage early or prompt payment. For example, increase your prices by 5% and then offer a 5% discount for payment within x number of days. Those customers that pay on time won't mind becasue they won't lose out. Also, consider exercising your legal right to charge a penalty interest for late payment.

Do a credit check — if a customer is likely to buy a lot from you then make sure you check them out thoroughly before doing business. Do not assume they are credit worthy. If a high value customer lets you down then you are going to struggle; non-payment or late payment of a significant invoice could have a huge effect on your cash flow and might force you under. So, do not take on customers on trust. Get an online credit rating by paying a credit reference agency such as Experian or Equifax for an instant company search.

Include a retention of title clause — if you provide stock to a company you should consider including a retention of title clause in your Terms and Conditions. This means that if the customer fails to pay in full for goods supplied, you have a right to repossess them, i.e. you retain title ownership over the goods even though they have physically passed to the buyer. As the law relating to this is ever changing it is advisable to seek appropriate legal advice when drafting such a clause.

Send out invoices promptly — sending out invoices on time is critical to maintaining cash flow. Do not give customers the impression that it doesn't matter when they pay. Chase up overdue payments politely but firmly both in writing and by phone. Bank all cheques and cash immediately.

Keep proper records — if you have a few major customers keep separate records for each, detailing: what you have sold to them, how much they owe and when they pay. Use this information to work out which are 'good' payers and which are poor and need watching.

> *Money flows are not something that just happen – you control them.*

Control your expenditure

Manage your suppliers — in all likelihood you will have a few key suppliers so try to arrange with these to have payments spread for large one-off purchases. If this is not possible then negotiate the best deal you can and do not pay until you have to. You may also be able to negotiate discounts for certain purchases. Get to know your suppliers and establish a good working relationship so that you become a valued customer to them.

Consider leasing rather than buying — rather than buying outright. If you don't have the funds to buy outright, leasing cars, vans and office equipment will help spread payments over the year. However, make sure you read the small print carefully of any lease agreement so that you do not get hit with any unexpected charges.

4.6 Using Your Cash Flow

As you update your cash flow with actual figures you will need to adjust your future estimates in the light of what you are discovering, so your cash flow will be a dynamic document, something that you will use to decide whether your business is on track as planned or whether there are steps you should take to bring it back in line. For example, you may decide that you need to increase your overdraft for a period and arrange this with your bank manager or you may decide to bring forward an advertising campaign to boost sales. Alternatively, if you are doing better than planned you may decide to put some spare cash into a higher interest account or invest in short term investments. Your bank manager will be able to advise.

4.7 Break-even Point

Your break-even point is achieved when your sales income reaches the level at which it covers start up, variable costs, fixed costs and your personal survival income.

A simple calculation at the outset will give you a good indication of whether or not your business is ever likely to be profitable.

> *Some businesses simply will never sell enough to make a profit, they will never reach their break-even point, and so will fail right from the start.*

To calculate your break-even point start with these 3 steps:

1. Decide what your 'unit' of sale will be; it could be one item of your product or one hour, or one day's worth of your time, if you're providing a service. Whatever you use, you must be able to put a value to it. Let's say that one unit of your product might sell for £15.

2. Work out your variable costs to provide one unit; remember, these are costs related specifically to providing one unit of sale such as material, labour and delivery costs. In this example we'll say they are £10.

3. Work out your fixed monthly costs; for example: rent, business rates, electricity, stationery and other business expenses, plus your personal survival income. Let's say these are £1,000 per month.

You will see from the above that each sale of £15 would make £5(*£15-£10*) towards paying your fixed costs of

£1,000 per month. If each sale contributes £5 toward your fixed costs, you would need to sell £1,000 ÷ 5 = 200 units per month in order to break even. This can be shown as the following formula:

Break-even point =

$$\frac{\text{Fixed costs (per month)}}{\text{Sale price of 1 unit minus the average variable cost of producing 1 unit}}$$

So, selling 200 units per month would enable you to break even in that month; however, you might aim to sell 500 units per month. Once you have the information from steps 1-3 above, you can estimate whether your expected level of sales will produce a profit or not. Let's see how the above translates into a financial summary:

In one month you plan to sell 500 units at £15 each	£7,500.
Take away the variable costs of producing those sales, (i.e. 500 x £10)	£5,000.
Which leaves a profit before fixed costs of 1/3 of sales value (i.e. your variable costs are 2/3 of the selling price)	£2,500.
Take away your fixed costs for one month	£1,000.
Which leaves your profit	£1,500.

Try to get a feel for these figures and be aware of how your variable and fixed costs will affect your profitability. By doing this you will soon begin to understand how important it is to keep a tight control over your costs.

> *High fixed costs are one of the main reasons many small businesses fail. Always think of ways to control your costs and how to keep them as low as possible.*

Working out your monthly personal survival budget

Use **Table 4** as an example, to work out what it costs you to live each month, then you will know how much money your business needs to make and what you will need to take in drawings each month.

T.4 Sam's Personal Survival Income

Estimated monthly living costs	£
Rent/Mortgage	800
Water Rates	25
Council Tax	90
Electricity/Gas	100
Food/household bills	450
Clothes	100
Car tax/maintenance (personal use)	50
Car petrol/diesel	100
Telephone/mobile	40
Family expenditure (children's expenditure, other dependants, social life e.g. meals out, drinks, clubs)	145
Holidays	nil
Home entertainment	nil
Subscriptions (magazines, leisure clubs)	nil

Credit cards/other personal loan repayments	20
Savings Plan	nil
Dental/medical	nil
A. ESTIMATED TOTAL MONTHLY LIVING COSTS	1,920
Monthly Income	
Working tax credits	nil
Income from partner/family members	1050
Child Benefits(s)	80
Pension/investments	nil
Other income	nil
B. TOTAL	1,130
SURVIVAL INCOME (drawings needed from business = A − B)	790

See over for: Sam's Cash Flow Forecast

Cash Flow Forecast For 12 Months Ending: 5/4/2014						
Month	Pre	Apr	May	Jun	Jul	Aug
	0	1	2	3	4	5
Quantity Of Sales						
Cash In						
Customers (Corporate)		400	2000	2000	3000	3000
Customers (Performers)				1000	1000	2000
Own Funds	1500					
Personal Loan	1500					
A Total Cash In	3000	400	2000	3000	4000	5000
Cash Out -						
Personal Drawings		800	800	800	800	1500
Casual Labour		100		200		300
Capital Expenditure	1000					
Supplies	300	250	250	300	400	500
Nhi (Staff & Personal)		12	12	12	12	12
Business Rent & Rates		120	120	120	120	120
Marketing & Advertising	250	50	50	50	250	100
Services (Electricty,Gas,Water)		15	15	15	15	15
Phone/Mobile	100	45	45	45	45	45
Post/Stationery		20	20	20	20	20
Business Insurance	205					
Publicl Liability Insurance	190					
Diesel		200	200	200	200	250
Vehicle Maintenance				60		
Loan Repayments		130	130	130	130	130
Legal/Professional				250		
Net Vat Payments						
Other Travel/Subsistence			150		150	
B Total Cash Out	2045	1742	1792	2202	2142	2992
Net Cash Flow In/(Out) [A-B]	955	-1342	208	798	1858	2008
Opening Balance/(Deficit)	0	955	-387	-179	619	2477
Closing Balance/(Deficit)	955	-387	-179	619	2477	4485

Pricing, Budgeting & Cash Flow 93

Business Name:			Sams View				
Sep	Oct	Nov	Dec	Jan	Feb	Mar	Totals
6	7	8	9	10	11	12	
							0
3500	3500	4000	3000	1000	2000	3000	30400
1500	1500	2000	2000	3000	1000	2000	17000
							1500
							1500
5000	5000	6000	5000	4000	3000	5000	50400
1500	1500	2000	2000	2000	2000	2000	17700
300	300	600	300			100	2200
500	500	400	400	400	400	300	4900
12	12	12	12	12	12	12	144
120	120	120	120	120	120	120	1440
50	50	50	50	50	50	50	1100
15	15	15	15	15	15	15	180
45	45	45	45	45	45	45	640
20	20	20	20	20	20	20	240
							205
							190
250	250	250	200	200	200	120	2520
60			60			60	240
130	130	130	130	130	130	130	1560
250			250				750
							0
150		150		150		150	900
3402	2942	3792	3602	3142	2992	3122	34909
1598	2058	2208	1398	858	8	1878	14491
4485	6083	8141	10349	11747	12605	12613	14491
6083	8141	10349	11747	12605	12613	14491	

YOUR NOTES

Chapter 5

Keeping Records

Chapter 5
Keeping Records

Whilst your cashflow forecast reflects your best estimate of how your business will perform over the forthcoming period, it's the records you keep that will tell you how you are actually doing on a monthly, weekly or even daily basis.

You probably know already that for tax purposes you must keep all your business invoices and receipts — and you may have been told that it's OK just to keep them in a shoebox or similar and present them to your bookkeeper or accountant at the end of the year to do your tax returns. But doing this and nothing else will cost you money. It will cost you because you will have to pay your bookkeeper to sort out your mess; it will cost you because you probably won't have much idea of whether all your customers have paid you all they owe; it will cost you if you have to borrow money in order to cover your future debts and it will cost you because you will have no idea as to whether the level of business you are achieving is enough to cover all your expenses.

> *Creating unnecessary costs for yourself does not make good business sense and could mean that you will soon join the 55% of small businesses that fail in the first year!*

Don't muddle through — that's no way to do business — instead, start by setting up a few simple records and get used to using this information to see how your business is doing and plan for the future.

5.1 HMRC

HMRC (Her Majesty's Revenue and Customs) is responsible for collecting and issuing taxes to ensure that money is available to fund the UK's public services. These include such areas as social protection (e.g. family benefits, pensions and sickness and disability payments); health, transport, education, defence, public safety and general public services such as recreation and culture. Let's look briefly at what HMRC require from you and how you will be taxed.

a) Registering with HMRC

Even if you already complete a tax return each year you need to let HMRC know as soon as possible that you have become self-employed. The HMRC tax year runs from 6 April one year until 5 April the following and at the latest you must register your self-employment status with them by 5 October following the tax year in which you started trading. So, for example, if you became self-employed during the tax year April 2013-2014 you need to let HMRC know by no later than 1 October 2014.

For details of how to register see HMRC's website https://online.hmrc.gov.uk/registration/newbusiness/introduction. When you register you will need:

❏ Your National Insurance number

- ❑ Your contact details and the contact details of your business (which may be the same)
- ❑ Your postcode and the name of your business. You may just use your own name if you haven't thought of a separate business name.
- ❑ The date you became self-employed (started trading).

HMRC will issue you with a ten-digit Unique Taxpayer Reference (UTR) number which you must keep safe. You will be able to use this to register for the free online service to allow you to complete your tax return online. They will also set up records for you to make sure you pay the right amount of tax and NI at the right time.

HMRC should notify you in April or May following your registration of when you need to do your first tax return.

Value Added Tax (VAT)

Currently the VAT registration threshold is £79,000 per annum. If your business takings from VAT taxable goods and services for the previous 12 months are greater than this amount, or if you expect them shortly to reach this threshold, then go to the HMRC website and click on 'VAT' to find out more and to register for VAT if applicable.

b) Accounting records

All businesses are required by law to keep what the law describes as proper and adequate financial records relating to it and retain these for six years. Even though as a sole trader you do not have to submit your accounts with your Self Assessment tax return you do have to be able to back up your figures if required. HMRC will also expect you to keep all business records, including bank statements, cheque stubs and paying-in books, mileage records and capital items bought for the business. Keep all business transactions separate from personal transactions by opening a bank account purely for your business. You will also need to keep a record of stock on hand at the accounting date, for example, 5 April.

c) The accounting period

You must decide on your 'accounting year' and this can be any date you choose. Regardless of when they start business, many people choose to match their accounting date to the end of the tax year, 5 April (mainly because it simplifies their understanding of how the tax system works). If you make this choice then your first year of business will start on the date you began business and end on 5 April. Each following year it will run from 6th April-5 April.

d) Calculating profit

As a self-employed person you pay tax on your profits, which includes the income you have paid yourself through personal 'drawings' from the business. So for each accounting period or year, you will need to prepare accounts for your business. These accounts will summarise income from your sales and all your costs (variable costs, fixed costs and in the first year your start-up costs) so as to arrive at your business profit.

One very important point to note is that, because these accounts must show what you have earned, they may include sales for which you have not yet received payment and costs which you have not yet paid. (This is different to your cashflow & cash book in which you do not show an amount until the money is received). Your ledgers, referred to in Section 5.2, will help you keep a record of your work and the invoices which you have issued and your purchases and invoices received for payment.

You may need to ask a reputable accountant or bookkeeper to prepare these accounts if you do not know how to do it yourself — don't forget to include the cost of this help in your fixed cost estimates and budgets.

e) Allowable expenses

When you are self-employed there are various business expenses you can claim, to help reduce your tax bill. For tax purposes, only allowable business expenses — costs incurred for the sole purpose of earning business profits — should be included in your costs (your own 'drawings' are not counted as an allowable expense and so cannot be deducted). Where expenses relate to both business and personal use only the business element is allowable. So, for example, if your office is a room in your house, your rent, rates, lighting and heating bills should be split and part of them designated as a business cost according to what proportion of your accommodation is used solely for business purposes. If you have bought any large capital items such as machinery or vehicles, or spent money on such items as the purchase or alteration of business premises these are not included as a business expense but recorded separately as assets of the business. For tax purposes you can claim an Annual Investment Allowance or Capital Allowance which will reduce your taxable profit. See: http://www.hmrc.gov.uk/incometax/relief-self-emp.htm for details of allowable & non-allowable expenses.

f) Income tax

As a self-employed person, income tax is payable on the profit your business makes, not the amount of money you take out of the business for your personal needs and use. You have to pay tax on the profit your business makes over a certain level. That level is known as your personal allowance — for 2013/14 this is £9,440 (for income up to £100,000). You pay tax only on profit above this amount. In 2013/14 you would have paid 20% on profit from £9,441 – £32,010 and 40% tax on profit over £32,011 per yr (up to £150,000) The personal allowance limits vary and are higher for those over 65 yrs. As these limits are revised every year it is worth checking current information on the HMRC website: www.hmrc.gov.uk/rates and look for income tax rates.

g) National Insurance

As a self-employed person you will normally pay Class 2 National Insurance at a fixed rate of £2.70 per week (2013/2014) AND Class 4 NIC of 9% if your profits are above the lower profit limit – £7,755 for 2013/2014.

h) Paying tax

HMRC issues SA316 — Notice to Complete a Tax Return — as soon as the tax year starts on 6 April. HMRC encourage you to make your return online but if you do not have this facility you can still make a paper return using the records you have kept throughout the year. You must file your return by 31 October if completed on paper or by the following 31st January if online. Either way you must pay the balance of any tax and Class 4 National Insurance you owe by 31 January and at the same time make your first payment on account for the following tax year. You must pay your second payment on account by 31 July.

If you are newly self-employed HMRC will set up your Self Assessment Online account automatically when you register for business taxes. To log in to your account online you will need the UTR which HMRC will have sent you, together with either your NI number or your postcode. As a sole trader you register as an 'Individual'.

As a general rule, as a minimum, put aside about 25% (1/4) of your profits each month into a separate account for tax and NI purposes.

It is a very good idea to put some money aside each month in order to have funds to pay your tax bill when it is due. Don't neglect this or the tax bill may come as a nasty surprise just when you thought you were doing OK!

5.2 Keeping Your Records

Tax returns won't be a problem if you keep some simple records. There are three basic sets of information you will find useful in order to manage your business. (If you employ staff you will also need a wages book):

- A record of your sales — known as the sales ledger.
- A record of your purchases — known as the purchase ledger.
- The cash book.

A 'ledger' simply means a book where you keep a record of your financial accounts.

Sales ledger and purchase ledger

You will use these two books to record all the work you have undertaken for which you will be paid and all the expenses you have incurred. These books will provide you with the information you need to do your tax return and your profit and loss statement.

a) Sales ledger

Once you have made a sale, issue a numbered invoice and keep a copy. All invoices should show the following information:

INVOICE

- Date of the invoice.
- A reference number e.g. 001/13.
- Your business name and address.
- Name and address of the customer.
- A clear description of what you are charging for and when the goods or service were provided.
- The amount(s) being charged (the amount net of VAT plus the VAT = gross amount, if VAT registered).

A simple way to keep all your records neat is to file the invoices you have issued in a ring binder, in date order, with the oldest at the back. If you make any cash sales then issue a numbered receipt and record and file these in the same way. Enter the details in your sales ledger as soon as you have completed the work and issued the invoice.

An extract from an example Sales ledger for 'Sam's View' is shown at **Table 6 (T.6)**. He is not VAT registered and so does not need to include any figures in the VAT columns. You can have one column for when you issue the invoice and another for when you actually receive the money — that way you can keep tabs on who has not paid you and chase it up. From this example of 'Sam's View' you will see that J Frampton and Soloquest have not yet paid their invoices — and so perhaps need a reminder!

T.6　Sales Ledger

Customer Details	Invoice Number /2013	Date of Invoice /2013	Net of VAT Total	VAT	Gross Total	Date invoice paid (transferred to cash book)
J. Frampton	018	26/04			390.00	
P. Floweth	019	01/05			325.00	07/06
P. Floweth	020	03/05			300.00	14/06
J. Goulding	021	03/05			600.00	11/06
Soloquest	022	06/05			120.00	
J. Brown	023	14/05			425.00	07/06

b) Purchase ledger

Your purchase ledger records expenses that you have incurred on behalf of your business. You enter the information into the ledger as soon as you have incurred the expenditure and not when you actually pay for the item or service. Give the invoices you receive a number e.g. P6/P7 and file them in a ring binder in numerical order with the oldest at the back. If they're fiddly, you could use a system whereby you have a plastic wallet for each month; start by labelling March at the back and go through to April. Put each invoice in the appropriate wallet in the ring binder. Enter the details into your purchase ledger following the example given for 'Sam's View'. (See T.7). (If you are VAT registered you should add two further columns to show expenditure net of VAT and VAT).

Sam has decided that his main budget areas for expenditure are likely to be:

- Photographic supplies.
- Diesel and travel expenses.
- Marketing and Advertising.
- Rent and rates.
- Telephones and stationery.

He has drawn up a separate column for each in his purchase ledger so that he can keep an eye on how much he is spending in each area and at the end of every month he can compare his expenditure against his budget and cashflow estimate for that month. This is a good way to do business. At the beginning of the year you should have decided on your main budget areas, i.e. where your main costs are likely to be, and how much you are likely to spend in each area. Draw up columns in your purchase ledger to record amounts spent under each budget heading. This information will also help you with your tax return as these costs will be allowable expenses and you will be able to deduct the amounts you have spent from your taxable income. As with 'Sam's View' you should add another column for any other expenses e.g. Contractor Services. Additionally, you could add a final column detailing your personal drawings.

c) Cash book

Sales and purchase ledgers reflect all invoices issued by you, whether or not you have received the money yet, and all bills that you have received, whether or not you have yet paid them. Your cash book records actual monies received in and out of the business.

Record amounts in your cash book once your invoices are paid (income) or when you make a payment (expenditure). To keep these records you could use a cash book with Income on the left hand side and Expenditure on the right and total up and rule off at the end of every month. Alternatively, set up your own pages on a computer, using Excel, or use a readymade accounting package. You must decide which is best for you. Your cash book is your final record of all money coming into and going out of your business. It also records what you pay into the bank, what you take out of it and your petty cash. Below is an example of an extract from a cash book for 'Sam's View'. (See T8).

Your ledgers will ensure that you have a complete record of all your business activity.

Sam has made the payments shown in the Table. You will note from his purchase ledger that he has incurred other expenditure, e.g. he has received an invoice for a mail shot (P9) and one for his supplies (P10), which is not shown in his cash book because he has not yet issued a cheque or made a card payment for this expenditure. When he does he will enter the amounts into his cash book. Your cash book should help you to work out how much cash you have and whether your payments are exceeding your receipts. If you have a lot of outstanding debtors on your sales ledger you should take steps to make sure they pay before you find yourself in a cash crisis!

See over for Table 7.
"Purchase Ledger"

T.7 Purchase Ledger

Date June 2013	Invoice No.	Details	Purchases/expenditure Supplies	Diesel & Travel
1/6	P6	Rent		
3/6	P7	Contractor Services		
5/6	P8	Fuel		60.00
6/6	P9	Mail Shot		
11/6	P10	Photographic Supplies	310.00	
12/6	P11	Mobile Phone		
15/6	P12	Stationery		
16/6	P13	Fuel		60.00
17/6	P14	Film	15.00	
20/6	P15	Car Repairs		
24/6	P16	BT		
29/6	P17	Contractor Services		
30/6	P18	Fuel		70.00
Total			325.00	190.00

Keeping Records 111

| Purchases/expenditure |||| Date Paid |
Marketing & Advertising	Rent & Rates	Telephones & Office Costs	Other Allowable Expenses	
	120.00			1/6
			200.00	3/6
				5/6
125.00				
		35.00		18/6
		22.40		15/6
				16/6
			65.00	20/6
		15.00		
			145.98	30/6
				30/6
125.00	120.00	72.40	410.98	

T.8 Cash Book

Income						Expenditure					
Date	Invoice No.	Details	Type	Amount (£)	Date Paid Into Bank	Date	Ref No.	Supplier/ Payee	Type	Amount (£)	Petty Cah
7/6/13	023	J Brown	Cheque 012336	425.00	10/6/13	1/6/13	P6	R Briggs	Cheque 002564	120.00	
10/6/13	019	P Floweth	Credit Transfer	325.00	10/6/13	3/6/13	P7	S Jones	Cheque 002565	200.00	
11/6/13	-	Investment Interest		50.00	11/6/13	5/6/13	P8	Shell	Card	60.00	
11/6/13	021	J Goulding	Cheque 006782	600.00	13/6/13	15/6/13	P12	Viking	Card	22.40	
14/6/13	020	P Floweth	Credit Transfer	300.00	14/6/13	20/6/13	Pc				50.00

5.3 Bank Reconciliation

Make sure that you receive a bank statement for your business bank account once a month. Make time each month to check that all monies that you have paid into your bank account are recorded and that all cheques that you have written or other payments that you have made are also shown. There may be some discrepancies, for example, if you have paid for something by cheque which has not yet been presented by the receiver or if a cheque you have paid in has not yet gone through or has 'bounced'. To double check that your cash book and bank account agree you should do a bank reconciliation as soon as you have your bank statement to hand for that month. These are the steps to take:

- ❐ **NOTE** the end of month balance as per bank statement.

- ❐ **ADD** deposits you have made that are not shown on the statement.

- ❐ **DEDUCT** payments that you have made that are not shown on the bank statement.

Is the final figure the same as your cash book? If, 'yes' then you have reconciled your bank account with your cash book. Great! If 'no' then investigate further. For example, there may be bank charges on your bank statement that will not be included in your cash book or you may have received interest into your bank account that you did not know about. Add the receipts to, or deduct the payments from, your cash book balance.

5.4 Profit and Loss Account

Your cashflow forecast is a prediction of how you think your business will perform over a certain period and once you have received income or made expenditure you update it with the information. However, it is not an accurate picture of the value of your business over this period as there will be work that you have done for which you have not yet been paid, or costs that you have incurred that you have not yet met. Unlike your cashflow, your profit and loss calculations refer only to work done in that particular period.

Once you take these into account, together with an estimation of the amount of depreciation on your capital items (the loss in value each year of its useful life), then you will have a much truer picture of the profit or losses that your business is making. Providing you keep accurate sales and purchase ledgers and a cash book your bookkeeper or accountant will be able to draw up a profit and loss statement for you.

5.5 Employing Workers

You may want to have people working **for** you as employees, or **with** you on a self-employed basis. If they work for you then you will need to register with HMRC, list them on your payroll and set up a PAYE scheme. If they have self-employed status then you do not need to do this, but you still need to keep clear records of all payments made to them and for what purposes.

Whether or not a worker is classed as an employee depends on a number of factors to do with the nature of the contract you have with them and the amount of control you have over such things as how, when and where the work is carried out and how the worker is paid by you. The HMRC website gives clear advice on this so, for further information, go to www.hmrc.gov.uk/calcs/esi.htm and use the 'Employment Status Indicator' tool.

If you decide to employ someone there are a number of actions you must take:

- It is your responsibility as the employer to check that the worker is legally allowed to work in the UK. For more information go to: www.gov.uk/legal-right-work-UK and use the quick check tool.

- You must register with HMRC as an employer and set up a PAYE scheme. Use the HMRC's software or a good 3rd party program like Payroll Manager to take care of online filing.

- Ensure that you have adequate Employers' Liability insurance. (See: www.gov.uk/employers-liability-insurance). This is a legal requirement and will provide insurance cover if an employee becomes ill or injured as a result of the work they do for you.

- Give your employee(s) a written statement concerning the main terms and conditions of employment, within two months of their starting work with you. Further guidance on this can be found on the 'ACAS' webiste at: www.acas.org.uk and search for 'written statement'.

YOUR NOTES

Chapter 6

Your Business Plan

Chapter 6
Your Business Plan

It is through doing the activities described in this book that you will gather the information you need for your business plan. Writing down a business plan will help you pull it all together and will reassure any potential investors that you have thought about the different elements of doing business and are aware of, and have addressed, potential problems. In it you should explain what you want to achieve and how you are going to achieve it. If you are applying for outside funding or a loan your plan must cover all of the aspects in reasonable detail; if the amount you need to borrow is substantial then you will need greater detail with complete financial projections.

However, for your own purposes writing a simple business plan to start with will help you move your ideas forward and gain a true sense of whether or not you have a feasible business. It will assist you in putting the building blocks in place so that you go in the right direction; so that you don't waste money on false leads or fantasies and to help you focus on the skills you will need in order to create a successful business and then grow that business.

6.1 Why Have A Business Plan?

There are two very good reasons for taking time to write a business plan:

- It will help you gather your thoughts and bring together in one place all the different pieces of information you have. As you write it you must be truthful with yourself and analyse whether you really do have a solid business idea. Take action to put right any shortfalls in your plan.

- If you need to apply to a funding body, such as a bank or other organisation, for a loan for the business they will want to see your business plan. They will only lend to businesses that stand a good chance of being able to repay the loan, so your business plan must convince them of this.

> **Statistics show that over half of small businesses in the UK fold within the first year. You do not need to be one of these.**

The main reasons for failure are:

- Lack of planning and research — working through a business plan will help ensure you do not fail for these reasons. You must be sure there is sufficient demand for your product or service and that you can sell at a profit.

- Cash flow — late payments by customers threaten the future of your business. However, by keeping accurate records — a sales ledger, a purchase ledger and a cashbook — and updating your cash flow at the end of every month, you need not fall into this trap.

❐ Marketing — many small businesses do little or no marketing and when they do advertise it may not reach those customers who are likely to buy the product or services. A simple marketing plan will help you 'sell' the benefits of your business to the right customers at the right time and in the right place.

❐ General management skills — you may not have all the skills you need and if you do not recognise this then you may be incapable of managing your business. If you find yourself in this situation either acquire the skills or knowledge yourself (remember there are a lot of free short business-related courses on offer) or find someone who can do the work for you, for example, a bookkeeper. Whichever solution you choose, don't ignore the issue.

Many sole traders fail because they lack sufficient funds to carry on their business. Paying close attention to the above areas could help you avoid a similar pitfall.

By grasping and understanding the reasons for failure you can take steps to avoid them and improve your chances of success. For an excellent example of a business plan for a sandwich selling company see the Sage, in association with Lloyds Bank, web page at http://businesshelp.lloydsbankbusiness.com/assets/pdf/Example-Business-Plan.pdf. You can also view sample business plans online. See: www.bplans.com.

6.2 Applying For Funding

Sources of funding

Over the last few years, the prevailing economic climate has made it very difficult for new and small businesses to get business loans. Family and friends may be willing to help out, but of course, not all are in a position to do so or you may not want to take advantage of this source. But, the bottom line is that you will need some funding to get going and to see you through the early months before your business starts to make a profit. Even if you do not require much stock or many materials up front you will, nevertheless, have bills to meet during the start-up phase and you must be realistic about this and estimate what your financial need will be.

But all is not doom and gloom; there are various sources you can apply to for support and some avenues to follow are listed below. In doing so, it is worth noting that all providers of funding, almost without exception, will undertake a credit check on you, they will require you to have a convincing business plan (although some may help you to complete this), and a cash flow forecast. All lenders will require you to repay the loan with interest, although the amount of interest they seek will vary from lender to lender. So, do not go into this lightly and if you take up a loan make sure you include within your cash flow the repayments you will need to make each month over the period of the loan.

- **The 'Funding for Lending Scheme'** is an initiative by the Bank of England, to encourage high street banks to lend money (which, as we all know, they have been very reluctant to do over recent years) to people wanting mortgages and to provide credit for small businesses. Initially, this scheme has been quite successful in stimulating the mortgage market, but has not done much for small businesses. Hopefully, this is about to change as, with effect from January 2014, it has been announced, the focus will be on supporting small businesses. So, although you may have been reluctant to do so in the past, in future it may be worthwhile making an appointment with you bank's business adviser to explore possible funding options.

- **Business Start-Up Loans** are aimed at those who have a feasible business idea but no access to funding. The loan is a personal loan to help you start your business and if successful, you will also be linked up with a business mentor. The Start-Up Loans Company (part of the Department for Business Innovation and Skills) uses a network of organisations throughout the UK to deliver the programme. The average loan is now about £5,500 and you will be charged interest on the loan (currently 6% fixed rate), which you will pay back over 1-5 years. For further information and to apply go to www.startuploans.co.uk

- **New Enterprise Allowance** is for those who receive certain state benefits to help them set up in business. As part of this scheme you will receive a weekly allowance and be able to apply for a loan and mentor support through the 'Start-Up Loan' scheme. Talk to your local Job Centre Plus advisor to check your eligibility and for further information.

❐ **Community Development Finance Institutions (CDFIs).** There are currently about 60 CDFIs supporting small businesses across the UK which have particular interests in developing businesses within their local area. They lend to those who might otherwise find it difficult to borrow from traditional sources or who live in deprived areas. Each organisation will have its own terms and conditions but they all will charge a lower interest rate than loan sharks or doorstep lenders. Go to www.findingfinance.org.uk to find out more and to get the names of your local CDFIs.

There are of course other projects, such as The Prince's Trust for 18-30 year olds, and other sources of finance and support, which you could explore. Contact details for some of these are given at the end of chapter 1 under 'Resources'. Business Link, now defunct, produced an excellent funding guide for small business and although it does not contain up to date information regarding current incentives it is still worth reading for the general advice which it gives. It is still available at: www.businesslink.gov.uk/Finance_files/SBFcomplete2008.pdf

Business Plan Template

An example of the headings you could use for your plan are given below (Table 9) together with the main points you should include under each heading. You will see that just about everything has already been covered somewhere in the book.

When writing your business plan write as simply as possible, keeping your paragraphs short and using bullet points to highlight lists. Make it easy for the reader to follow your logic as you lay down your case before them; don't befuddle them!

The Business Plan is both an historical document - laying out what you have discovered and achieved so far - and a forward looking document - detailing what you intend to do in the future. Your future plans must be based on sound evidence; this is what potential investors in your business will be looking for. They will want to see your commitment, in terms of your time and financial investment (if possible) before they are willing to invest in you.

T.9 The Business Plan

SECTION 1 – BUSINESS AND PERSONAL CONTACT DETAILS

Business name, address, telephone number, email address – & website if available

Name and address of owner – i.e. your name, address, telephone number(s) and email address

Details of your business bank account – name and address of your bank and name of your business account advisor

Your skills and experience and any relevant qualifications which make you competent to run this business

SECTION 2 – BUSINESS DESCRIPTION

Give a succinct description of your business. Think back to your 30 second pitch (Section 3.3) and explain in a couple of sentences:

What you do and where you are based

Who your customers are

What makes you special (your USP)

Benefits to your customers

The state of the wider market and the opportunities this presents to you.

SECTION 3 – MARKET ANALYSIS

Think back to your market research and say what you have discovered about:

Your customers. Give the profile of your 'typical' customer(s). You may have more than one group.

Your competitors. Be realistic about the strengths and weaknesses of each main competitor and explain how you know that your 'offer to customers' better matches customer needs than your competitors'.

The state of the wider market and how you can take advantage of what's happening. This will help you demonstrate that you have thought about longer-term opportunities.

Say how and where you have gathered this information and give sources of evidence (e.g. statistical reports, surveys, web sites etc).

Conclude with a sentence or two explaining why customers will buy from you rather than elsewhere.

SECTION 4 – YOUR MARKETING PLAN

If you did some of the activities discussed in Section 3.5-3.8 of this book then you will have the information to hand for this part of your business plan. Gather this together and say:

What your market research has told you about the type of marketing your customers will respond to.

What marketing you are going to do, especially initial marketing to get the business off the ground; then what ongoing marketing you propose in the future to promote your business.

When you are going to carry out any particular advertising campaigns.

What costs are involved and what your marketing budget will be.

What you hope to achieve over the next 1-3 years in terms of new customers and repeat customers.

How you will monitor success, i.e. how will you know whether a particular marketing tool has worked?

Provide a link to your website if you have one.

SECTION 5 – OPERATIONAL DETAILS

This section includes the logistics of the business. Include information on:

Key suppliers. If you produce goods or offer a service where you have to buy in supplies then give details of your main supplier(s) and the reasons why you chose them over others.

Delivery to customers. Explain how you plan to get your goods to customers, for example say which courier service or delivery company you will use and why. What promises you make regarding delivery times, costs and your refund policy.

Explain what payment options you will offer customers and your payment terms and conditions.

Legal requirements – For example, confirm what insurances you need and that they will be in place, the insurance company used and cost. Describe any particular health and safety requirements and how you will meet these. Give details of patents/trademarks applied for if applicable.

SECTION 6 – FINANCIAL PROJECTIONS

You've done your cashflow, keep this in front of you as you explain this section.

Sales forecast. Give details of your expected monthly sales, any seasonal fluctuations and what growth you expect over the first 3 years of business. Say how you have arrived at your figures (See Section 4.3).

Costs. Summarise your costs under:

- **Start** Up Costs
- **Overheads** or Fixed Costs
- **Variable** or Direct Costs

Fixed Assets. In this section also give details of any big purchases you will be making which will become 'fixed assets' i.e. you will keep them in the business and not sell them on.

Funding – Once you have worked out your costs, estimated your sales and calculated your cashflow forecast you will have an idea of what funding, if any, you need to get started and to see you through the early phase of your business. Summarise any funds that you are bringing to the business and any other investments or loans which will bring money into the business at the start up. If you are looking for further investment then state clearly how much you require and for what period.

Pricing – Say what you will charge for your product(s) or service(s). Explain how you arrived at these figures e.g. based on what your competitors are charging and taking into account your costs.

Cash flow – refer to your cashflow which should be attached as an Appendix and explain any anomalies or uncertainties.

Your Break-even point – do the sums and explain.

APPENDICES

- ❏ **Start** Up costs
- ❏ **Personal** survival Income
- ❏ **Cash** flow forecast – 3 yrs
- ❏ **Profit** and Loss Account

6.3 Executive Summary

Once you have written your business plan you should prepare a short summary of it which you attach to the front of the plan. This is so that any busy executives, such as your bank manager, can assess very quickly whether or not your business is one in which they might be interested. You can summarise any figures in this section without explaining these. Follow this format giving about a paragraph on each section:

- ❏ Description of your business — name, location, product or service.
- ❏ Financial summary — how much you have already invested in the business and, if applying for funding, how much money you need and when will this be repaid.

❒ Customer focus — customer profile and explain your Unique Selling Point.

❒ Opportunities and threats — your analysis of your strengths and weaknesses compared with your competitors.

❒ Long term vision — impress your reader with an inspiring vision for your business.

6.4 Staying Legal

Although it is easy to start up as a sole trader there are some legal requirements which may apply to your particular business. Work through the checklist on the next page; it covers the main areas you need to think about.

T.10 Legal Checklist:

Topic	Checked
Licences — Some types of business require licences, for example if you are working with children, if you sell alcohol, or are dealing with food. Check with your Local Authority, Trade or Professional Association to make sure you have the required licences to do business. You can also check GOV UK, which has an online regulation checklist that you can work through to find out which regulations are likely to apply to you. Go to www.gov.uk Select 'Business and Self-employed' and then choose: Licences and licence applications and click on 'Licence Finder'. information.	
Health and Safety (H&S) — there are several areas of H&S legislation that apply to businesses, no matter what their size. If you employ staff you must be especially attentive to ensuring they operate in a safe working environment. This duty also extends to visitors to the workplace such as customers and suppliers. The H&S Executive website has lots of useful information, fact sheets and resources you can order. Go to www.hse.gov.uk/getting-started/index	
Opening a business bank account — you should keep your business finances separate from your personal money. The British Bankers Association offers a 'Business Account Finder' service for small businesses. Go to: www.bba.org.uk and look for 'Business Account Finder' then click on the live link for further information.	

Topic	Checked
Data Protection — the gathering and holding of personal data is tightly regulated. It includes rules such as ensuring that you have a person's consent before processing information about them, only keeping relevant, accurate and timely information and ensuring that it is stored securely. These principles apply to all databases, whether computerized or manual. If you keep a computer database you may also be required to notify the Information Commissioner so that your name can be added to the public register of data controllers. For further information go to: www.ico.gov.uk	
Intellectual Property — patents, trademarks, copyright and designs — Most sole traders will not be concerned with obtaining patent protection for their product or idea. However, if you do wish to protect some aspect of your business then you should investigate further. Some intellectual property rights are automatic, whilst others require a registration process before they become legally enforceable. If registration is required make sure that you register your IP concept before you disclose any details publicly. Always keep records of your work and add your name and date to these. As IP registration is complicated you will need the services of a registered patent or trademark agent to ensure that your work is legally protected. See www.ipo.gov.uk for more information and for registering a trademark.	

Topic	Checked
Your Trading Name — if you intend to operate as a sole trader using a name other than your own, there is a legal requirement for the name and address of the owner to be displayed at your business premises and on your business stationery. The Companies Act 2006 sets out the requirements regarding the use of business names. This part of the Act will apply to you if you use a name that is not your normal surname (with or without initials). For example if a person called Jenny Smith is a photographer and trades as Jenny Smith or J. Smith she is not affected by the Act. However, if she trades as Jenny Smith Photographer then the Act applies. You can get free advice on business names from Companies House See: www.companieshouse.gov.uk	
Solicitors — you may decide that you would like some legal advice to help with such things as contracts, offering personal guarantees, health and safety law, debt collection, product protection and so on. You could start by going to the Lawyers for Business website: www.contactlaw.co.uk. Experienced staff can offer you free advice over the phone and put you in touch with the right solicitor for your needs from their register of solicitors.	
Register with HMRC — you must register with HMRC www.hmrc.gov.uk for tax and National Insurance purposes as soon as you start to trade.(See Chapter 5).	

Topic	Checked
Insurances — Make sure you provide adequately for any unforeseen circumstance through having the correct business insurances. Also, be aware, some insurances are compulsory for businesses. To get some guidance on which insurances you might need you could go to www.hiscox.co.uk/business-insurances. Some insurances you should consider are: *Employers' Liability* — If you employ staff you should check out the Health and Safety Executive's 'Employers' Guide' See www.hse.gov.uk/simple-health-safety/simplehealthsafety.pdf *Motor Insurance* — check with you insurance company that your insurance covers business use. If you use your car or van to transport goods for your business then you will need to buy a separate insurance policy *Public Liability Insurance* — covers you if someone sues you for injury to themselves or damage to their property caused in the course of your work. *Property and Stock Insurance* — check your property insurance to make sure that all machinery, stock, tools, equipment etc are covered. Look for an 'all risks' clause. *Professional Indemnity* — this is relevant if you provide advice such as accountants and business advisers. It covers legal liability for professional errors or omissions.	

6.5 Learn As You Go

Once you're up and running you'll be on a steep learning curve. Within 6 months of starting your business you'll know a huge amount more than you do now. Take time to look over your business plan and adjust your ideas according to what you have learnt.

> *You'll have discovered a lot along the way – so make the most of it and don't stand still!*

Running your own business will make demands on you and challenge you to do things you probably would avoid if it weren't for the fact that you are now responsible for the success or failure of your business.

By putting yourself in this position you may surprise yourself by finding new skills and talents that you weren't previously aware you possessed. Try to recognise where your talents lie, build on them and gain self-confidence from using and developing them. Of course, there will be areas where you are weak — but recognising where these areas are is a skill in itself — no one is good at everything, but the most successful people realise what they need help with and then go and find that help.

> *May I wish you every success in your business venture!*

YOUR NOTES

Index

A

accounts 99
  accounting period 99
  bank reconciliation 113
  records 98
  software 73, 115
    Money Manager 82
advertising
  AIDA 64–65
  effective 67
  online 65–66
advice and support 15–19, 67, 123
assets 100, 128
attitude 3
  to spending 17

B

bank 72, 121
  account 99, 125, 131
  reconciliation 113
benefits (to customers) 53
brand 33, 69, 79
breakeven point 89
British Chambers of Commerce 18
budgets 84, 100

business
  acumen 4–6, 15
  ideas 13
  model 33–34, 74
  name 125, 133
  plan 12, 44, 118–120, 123–124
  targets 11

C

cashbook 120
cashflow 75, 83, 85, 106, 114
cashflow forecast 75, 96, 114, 128
communications 22
Companies House 133
competitive advantage 61
competitors 39, 55, 61
conversion Rates 67
costs 72–73, 88, 90, 96, 99, 128
  fixed 74–75
  start-up 73–74
  variable 73, 81, 88, 89, 99
credit checks 17, 35, 85, 121
credit reference agencies 17–18, 86
customer
  care 67–68
  legal rights 68
  loyalty 62–63

D

data
  analysis 41, 126
  protection 68, 132
debt 17–18
discount (to customers) 67, 85
drawings 75, 84, 90, 91, 99, 100, 107

E

earnings 46
employing people 114–115
entrepreneurs 2, 3, 7
executive summary 129
expenditure, estimated 75
expenses, allowable 100

F

failure, reasons for 119–120
family 90, 121
focus groups 39–40, 43
funding 118, 119, 121–123, 128, 129

G

gap in the market 13–15, 30–31
goals 11–12
Government 16
growth
  grow your business 3, 7, 81

H

Health & Safety 131, 134

HMRC
  National Insurance 101–102
  paying tax 101–102
  records required 98, 102–104
  registering with 97–98

I

image 60, 61, 69, 79
insurance 115, 127, 134
intellectual property 61, 132
internet 42–43
  resources 18–21

L

leasing 87
ledgers 102–104
  purchase ledger 106–107
  sales ledger 103–104
legal checklist 131–134
libraries, using 40, 42
licences 131
loans 19, 121–124

M

management 39, 120
market
  reports 41
  research 6, 31, 32, 37, 45, 46, 55, 63, 64, 77, 78, 80, 126
  size 46
marketing 120
market research 36
  analysis 41, 126, 130
  desk-based 40

focus groups 43
primary 36
questionnaires 37
test marketing 43, 44
trade fairs 40
motivation 2–3, 11

N

National Insurance (NI).
  See HMRC
networking 16

O

opportunities 4, 33, 55–56, 66
outgoings 83
overdraft 74, 84, 87
overheads 36, 75, 83

P

personal development plan 10–13
pitch, "thirty-second" 55–57, 125
price(s) 5, 30, 33, 46, 76–78, 89
purchase ledger. *See* ledgers

Q

questionnaires. *See* Market-
  Research

R

receipts 96, 108, 113
resources 18–21, 131

S

sales, estimating 79–81
self-employed, registering as 97
skills 6–8, 22, 120, 125, 135
social networking 42, 66
sole proprietor. *See* sole trader
sole trader 6, 16, 98, 102, 130, 133
solicitors 133

T

tax. *See* HMRC
test marketing. *See* market research
trademark 15, 61, 132
trading name 133

V

Value Added Tax (VAT) 98, 103,
  104, 106

"A useful and very readable guide for anyone contemplating setting up a small business, and will be a most welcome help to those already up and running"

Lymington Times

"This handy book is the best and simplest guide that I have come across to enable anyone with ambition to transform their dreams into reality."

Alan Blair MBE

"Sue Hunter has such a comprehensive and complete grasp of her subject that she is able to communicate her ideas with commendable simplicity. Her literary style flows effortlessly excluding no one from benefiting from the wealth of her experience. It is an indispensable guide for anyone who has the courage, but lacks the knowledge, to go it alone and set up their own business. For them it should be mandatory reading."

F. Rayner — former Dean of Studies at the National Radio, Television and Communications Centre at Hatch End.

Also available as an ebook at:
www.dashhousepublishing.co.uk